from Nonnie's Italian Kitchen

The Recipes of Mary Baldini Leonardi

Compiled and edited by
Elmerina Leonardi Parkman
Norma Leonardi Leone

Lion Press
Rochester, New York

First printing October, 1988
Second printing April, 1989
Third printing June, 1993

From Nonnie's Italian Kitchen

Copyright © 1988 by Lion Press

All rights reserved. No part of this book may be reproduced or transmitted in any form or by any means, electronic or mechanical, including photocopying, recording, or by any information storage and retrieval system, without permission in writing from the publisher, with the exception of brief quotations for review.

Inquiries should be addressed to:

> Lion Press
> P. O. Box 92541
> Rochester, NY 14692

Cover photographs by Paul Parkman
Black and white photographs by Tony Leone
Cover and Graphics by Natalie L. Schwartz
Typesetting and Design by Sasha Trouslot, Foxglove Graphics
Electronic editing by Tony Leone III

Library of Congress Cataloging-in-Publication Data

Leonardi, Mary B.
    From Nonnie's Italian Kitchen
    Includes index.
    1. Cookery, Italian. I. Parkman, Elmerina Leonardi, date. II. Leone, Norma Leonardi, date. III. Title.
TX723.L45   1988   641.5945   88-13414
ISBN 0-936635-25-8

Printed in the United States of America

For
Nonnie's Grandchildren

Christina and Tony

Ezio, Joseph, Mary and Theresa

Jacques, Nanette and Salvatore

For our parents, Mary and Salvatore Leonardi, with love and admiration, and our brothers, Ezio, Robert and Salvatore, Jr.

and with very special thanks to those who have joined our family, especially our husbands,

Paul and Tony,
and to

Barbara
Beatrice
Jim
Michelle

who love good food, prepared the Italian way.

Acknowledgments

We are deeply grateful to the many people who helped with this book. We especially thank our aunts, Teresa Leone, Rita Consalvi, and Martje Baldini; our cousins, Mary and Sal D'Aura, Betty Molella and Annita DeSantis; and our dear friends, Lena Rossi, Ella Pensone, Elena Vitagliano, and Jeneane Dimino.

Contents

INTRODUCTION	ix
SOUPS, SANDWICHES, AND PIZZAS	1
PASTA, RICE, AND SAUCES	15
CHICKEN, MEAT, AND SEAFOOD	35
VEGETABLES	59
SALADS	89
SWEETS AND FRUITS	99
LEONARDI'S RESTAURANT	125
LEONARDI'S RECIPES	129
TRADITIONAL HOLIDAY MENUS	135
INDEX	141

Introduction

The idea for this book began with a desire to preserve our mother's recipes for her grandchildren, who call her "Nonnie," a childhood interpretation of the Italian word for grandmother.

Everyone who knows our mother, Mary Leonardi, also knows she is a wonderful cook and that traditional Italian cooking is a very important part of her life. Her recipes reflect the influence of her parents, who came to America from Carpineto, a small village in the central hills of Italy, and of our father's family in Terracina, a seacoast town south of Rome, where he was born and lived until he came to America.

After 57 years of married life, our mother still prepares three meals a day and has a garden where she raises all her own parsley, oregano, basil and many vegetables. She buys garlic by the pound, oil by the gallon, and canned tomatoes by the case, which she uses to cook large quantities of food in preparation for visits from family and friends.

"Nonnie" is an energetic, hardworking woman who is devoted to her family and who takes great pride and satisfaction in giving them good food to eat. She loves visitors and, in the Italian tradition, immediately offers coffee and cookies. Hardly anyone leaves empty handed, as she usually gives them something freshly made or picked from her garden. Over the years she has taken great delight in teaching family and friends how to prepare many of her recipes. Her patience is endless, and her understanding nature and kindness are well known.

Once we started to record these traditional recipes, we realized that they would appeal to many people. The ingredients are fresh, the recipes are easy to prepare, and the foods are tasty and nutritious. Most of the recipes have never been written down before and have come directly from watching and helping our mother prepare the food.

This cookbook is for beginning and experienced cooks. The recipes can easily be adapted for special tastes by increasing or decreasing the amount of seasonings. In this age of instant foods and frozen pizzas, FROM NONNIE'S ITALIAN KITCHEN is a refreshing change. Follow these recipes and you will be twice rewarded: You will eat well and your family and guests will love you.

E.L.P.
N.L.L.

1988

Soups Sandwiches & Pizzas

CHICKEN SOUP
(Brodo Di Pollo)

3 pounds stewing chicken, cut into pieces
6 quarts water
2 to 3 stalks celery, with leaves
1 carrot
1 small onion
1 fresh tomato, cut up,
   or ½ cup canned crushed tomatoes
1 tsp. salt
¾ to 1 cup small pasta (pastina)

Bring the water to a boil in a large (8 qt.) kettle. Add chicken and bring to a boil again. Lower heat, skim off foam and add the vegetables. Cover and simmer for about 3 hours, until chicken is thoroughly cooked.

Strain the soup. Remove skin and bones from chicken and discard. Cut chicken into small pieces and use for chicken salad, if desired. Discard the vegetables (they can be eaten, but are quite soft).

Bring about 2 quarts of the strained chicken broth to a boil and add ¾ to 1 cup pastina. Cook until al dente. Freeze the remainder of the soup or refrigerate for use later.

VARIATION: (MINESTRONE) This soup can be used as stock for minestrone. Add fresh vegetables and/or cooked fresh escarole to the soup and cook for 20 to 30 minutes. Then add the pastina or serve with just the vegetables and no pastina.

Also, "Beaten Eggs" can be added instead of pastina to the clear soup.

Serves 6 to 8.

CHICKEN SOUP WITH BEATEN EGGS
(Brodo Di Pollo Con Stracciatella)

2 eggs, well beaten
1 Tbsp. sifted flour
1½ quarts chicken soup
1 to 3 tsp. grated Romano cheese (optional)

Beat eggs with flour. Bring soup to a boil and add egg mixture, stirring rapidly with a fork. When the soup comes to a boil again, remove from heat.

To give the eggs a finer consistency, use an egg beater for a few minutes after removing from heat.

VARIATION: Add grated Romano cheese to the eggs before beating and then follow directions as above.

OR: pass the cheese to sprinkle on the soup, to taste.

Serves 4 to 6.

LENTIL SOUP
(Zuppa Di Lenticchie)

½ lb. lentils
2½ quarts cold water
3 Tbsp. oil
1 small onion, chopped
1 to 2 stalks celery, chopped
¼ cup chopped celery leaves
½ cup tomato puree
½ cup water

Sort lentils, rinse in water, and drain. Put the lentils in a large kettle, add the water, and bring to a boil. Turn down the heat so that the lentils simmer. Cover and cook for about 1½ to 2 hours, or until tender.

While the lentils are cooking, heat the oil in a small pan. Add the onion, celery and celery leaves. Cook about 10 minutes, stirring often. Add the tomato puree and ½ cup water and continue cooking for about ½ hour more, stirring occasionally.

Add the tomato mixture to the lentils during the last ½ hour of cooking. Season with salt and pepper to taste.

VARIATION: Add ½ cup of pasta, such as small shells or ditalini, and cook an additional 10 minutes, until the pasta is al dente.

Serves 6 to 8.

PEA SOUP
(Pasta E Piselli)

¼ cup oil
1 medium onion, chopped
1 stalk celery, chopped
2 Tbsp. chopped celery leaves
½ cup crushed tomatoes
1 can peas (16-17 oz.), including juice
2 cans water
½ cup small pasta, such as
    ditalini or small shells

In a large pan, heat oil, add onion and celery and saute until soft. Add celery leaves and crushed tomatoes and cook for 5 to 10 minutes.

Add the canned peas, then fill the can with water twice and add to the mixture. Stir well. Simmer for about 30 minutes.

Just before serving, add pasta and cook an additional 8 to 10 minutes, until pasta is al dente.

Serves 4 to 6.

MOZZARELLA SANDWICH
(Mozzarella In Carrozza)

2 eggs, beaten
8 slices day-old Italian bread,
 sliced ½" thick
4 slices mozzarella cheese,
 ¼" thick
½ cup oil

Dip one side of each slice of bread in beaten eggs and fry in hot oil until golden brown. Continue until all the slices have been fried (on one side only).

To make the sandwiches, place mozzarella slice between the fried sides of bread. Dip the outside of the sandwich in beaten eggs and fry on each side until golden brown.

Serves 4.

NONNIE SAYS,"This sandwich is very good for lunch, served with either a vegetable or salad and fruit for dessert."

OPEN FACED CHEESE SANDWICHES WITH FRESH TOMATO TOPPING

(Crustini Al Pizziaiolo Con Pomodori Freschi)

4 fresh, ripe tomatoes, or
   1 cup canned crushed tomatoes
2 Tbsp. chopped fresh parsley
2 Tbsp. chopped fresh basil
1 tsp. minced garlic
1 Tbsp. oil
½ tsp. salt
⅛ tsp. pepper
8 slices Italian bread, ½" thick
¼ to ½ lb. mozzarella cheese,
   sliced ¼" thick

Chop the tomatoes coarsely (and drain if watery). Add basil, parsley, garlic, oil, salt and pepper. Stir well.

Toast the bread lightly. Top each slice of bread with a slice of mozzarella cheese and toast again until the cheese is melted.

Pass the tomato mixture to put on top of the toasted bread and cheese.

VARIATION: After toasting bread, add seasoned tomatoes, top with a slice of mozzarella cheese, and toast again until cheese melts. Serve immediately.

Serves 4.

PIZZA DOUGH

(Impasto Per Pizza)

2¼ cups warm water
1 pkg. dry yeast
½ tsp. sugar
6 cups flour
¼ cup oil
1 tsp. salt

Pour ¼ cup warm water into a bowl and sprinkle with yeast and sugar. Stir well. When the yeast mixture foams (if it doesn't foam, yeast is not active and should be discarded), add about a cup of the flour and mix well. Then add 2 cups of warm water, the oil, remaining flour and salt. Mix well, turn out on a floured board and knead until smooth. Rub the surface of the dough with a little oil and place in a greased bowl. Cover and let rise in a warm place until double in bulk.

Divide dough into two pieces. Grease two 11 x 15" pans. Roll dough out or shape with hands to fit the pans. Cover and let rise a second time, until almost double in bulk.

Cover with seasoned tomatoes or use for any of the other pizza variations. Follow directions for each recipe for baking. Serve hot.

Serves 6.

SEASONED TOMATOES FOR PIZZA

1 28 oz. can crushed tomatoes
½ cup grated Romano cheese
1 tsp. salt
1 to 2 tsp. dried oregano, crushed
1 clove garlic, chopped finely
¼ cup oil
½ lb. mozzarella cheese,
   coarsely grated (optional)

Mix all ingredients except for mozzarella cheese. Spread evenly over pizza dough just before baking. Bake at 400° for about 30 to 45 minutes, or until dough is cooked and browned on the bottom. Remove from oven and sprinkle with mozzarella cheese, if desired. Bake until cheese melts (about 5 minutes).

CHEESE PIZZA
(Pizza Con Formaggio)

½ recipe pizza dough
½ to ¾ lb. provolone cheese,
    cut into ¼" thick slices
1 Tbsp. oil

Prepare pizza dough and roll out ½" thick. Place half the dough in an oiled 9 x 9" or 9" round baking pan.

Place sliced cheese on top of the dough. Cover with the remaining dough and squeeze edges together to seal the cheese in. Brush the top with oil.

Let rise until doubled. Bake at 400° for 20 to 30 minutes, until lightly browned.

Serves 4 to 6.

FRIED PIZZA DOUGH
(Pizze Fritte)

½ recipe pizza dough
1 cup oil
¼ to ½ cup sugar

Prepare pizza dough and let it rise. Punch the dough down and cut it into fist-sized pieces. Pour a little oil on your hands and then stretch each piece of dough until it is about ¼" thick and 6" in diameter.

Heat the oil in a deep pan and fry each piece until puffed and golden brown on both sides. Remove and drain on paper towels. Sprinkle the fried pizza with granulated or powdered sugar. Serve piping hot. Makes about 8 fried pizzas.

Serves 4 to 6.

WHITE PIZZA
(Pizza In Bianco)

½ recipe pizza dough
2 Tbsp. oil
1 tsp. oregano or rosemary
1 to 2 Tbsp. grated Romano cheese

Prepare pizza dough and let it rise. Punch down and roll out to ½" thickness. Place in an oiled baking pan (10 x 15").

Spread a thin coat of oil on top of the dough and sprinkle with grated Romano cheese and oregano or rosemary. Let rise a second time.

Bake at 400° for 30 minutes, or until lightly browned.

Serves 4 to 6.

Pasta Rice & Sauces

BAKED EGG NOODLES
(Pasta Di Uovo Al Forno)

1 lb. egg noodles, ½" wide or wider
1 lb. ricotta
¾ to 1 lb. mozzarella cheese
¾ to 1 cup grated Romano cheese

6 to 8 cups tomato sauce

Cook egg noodles in boiling salted water until firm (about 2 minutes). Drain lightly and add a small amount of sauce to keep the noodles from sticking together.

Pour a little sauce on the bottom of a 10 x 15" baking pan. Add a layer of egg noodles. Spoon some of the ricotta over the noodles. Then add chunks or slices of mozzarella and sprinkle with grated cheese. Add a layer of sauce and then continue making layers with the noodles and cheeses.

Top with a layer of sauce and sprinkle with grated cheese. Cover with foil and bake at 350° for about 35 to 45 minutes. Let the baked noodles stand for about 20 minutes before serving. Serve with extra sauce, if desired.

NOTE: This dish freezes well.

Serves 6 to 8.

BAKED PASTA
(Timballo)

1 lb. pasta, such as ziti or rigatoni
½ cup bread crumbs
½ cup grated Romano cheese
¼ lb. mozzarella cheese, sliced (optional)
4 cups tomato sauce

Cook pasta until firm (about 5 minutes) and drain. Mix 3 cups of the tomato sauce and ¼ cup of the grated Romano cheese into the pasta.

Grease a large casserole dish and sprinkle bottom and sides with half the bread crumbs. Pour the pasta into the casserole and cover with the remaining sauce. Sprinkle top with remaining bread crumbs and grated cheese. Top with mozzarella cheese, if desired.

Cover and bake at 325° for 20 minutes. Uncover and bake for an additional 10 minutes.

NOTE: This dish can be prepared ahead of time and baked just before serving. Leftover pasta can be used for this dish.

Serves 4 to 6.

MACARONI AND CHEESE
(Maccaroni E Formaggio)

½ pound elbow macaroni
1½ to 2 cups canned crushed tomatoes
2 Tbsp. oil
½ lb. mozzarella or process cheese, sliced
¼ cup bread crumbs (optional)

Cook elbow macaroni in boiling salted water until firm. Mix tomatoes with oil and season to taste with salt and pepper.

Put a small amount of tomato mixture on bottom of a well-greased baking dish. Add a layer of macaroni, tomato mixture and sliced cheese. Repeat until all ingredients are used, ending with a layer of tomatoes and cheese. Top with bread crumbs, if desired.

Bake, covered, for 20 minutes at 350°.

Serves 4.

PASTA WITH BROCCOLI
(Pasta Con Broccoli)

1 lb. broccoli
¼ cup oil
½ tsp. minced garlic
½ lb. ditalini, small shells or other small-sized pasta
Grated Romano cheese

Separate broccoli into florets and cook until tender. Drain, reserving water. Cook pasta until al dente.

Heat oil, add garlic and saute for about 10 to 20 seconds, stirring constantly. Add broccoli and saute for a few minutes, stirring gently. Add pasta and 1/2 cup reserved water (more if needed). Season with salt and pepper to taste and cook for about 3 to 5 minutes, until flavors are blended. Serve immediately. Pass grated Romano cheese to add as desired.

Serves 3 to 4.

NONNIE SAYS, "Cauliflower may be used in place of the broccoli, or a combination of broccoli and cauliflower is also very good."

POTATO DUMPLINGS
(Gnocchi)

2½ lbs. Idaho, Russet, or "old" potatoes
   (do not use "new" potatoes)
4½ cups flour (approximately)
1 egg, slightly beaten
2 tsp. salt
1 recipe spaghetti sauce
Grated Romano cheese

Wash potatoes and boil, with skins on, until tender. When cool, remove skins and put through a ricer (or mash them). Refrigerate potatoes to cool completely.

Put cold potatoes on a large board. Make a well in the center of the potatoes and add beaten egg, salt and about 1 cup of flour. Using your hands or a large spoon, mix well and continue to add flour until the dough is no longer sticky and can be kneaded like bread dough.

Cut off about ¼ of the dough. Roll out on a floured board to a thickness of about ½". Cut the rolled dough into strips, ½" wide. Then cut strips into ½" pieces. Spread pieces apart and roll each piece over tines of a fork to make ridges or the traditional shell shape. If necessary, sprinkle pieces with flour or dip tines of the fork in flour to keep the dough from sticking. OR: press your thumb into the center of each piece to make an indentation. After the pieces are shaped, put them on cookie sheets which have been lined with waxed paper and separate the pieces to keep them from sticking together. Repeat the process until all the dough has been used (shaping the gnocchi is usually a family affair, as many hands make it fun rather than work). Gnocchi do not keep well, so they should be cooked as soon as they are made.

TO COOK: Fill a large pot with water and bring to a rolling boil. Add 1 Tbsp. salt and the gnocchi. Stir constantly until the water comes to a boil. Continue boiling until gnocchi rise to the top of the water and are cooked (about 10 minutes). Drain, cover with tomato sauce and mix gently. Pass extra sauce and grated Romano cheese to add as desired.

Serves 4 to 6.

POTATO DUMPLINGS
(Gnocchi)

2½ lbs. Idaho, Russet, or "old" potatoes
   (do not use "new" potatoes)
4½ cups flour (approximately)
1 egg, slightly beaten
2 tsp. salt
1 recipe spaghetti sauce
Grated Romano cheese

Wash potatoes and boil, with skins on, until tender. When cool, remove skins and put through a ricer (or mash them). Refrigerate potatoes to cool completely.

Put cold potatoes on a large board. Make a well in the center of the potatoes and add beaten egg, salt and about 1 cup of flour. Using your hands or a large spoon, mix well and continue to add flour until the dough is no longer sticky and can be kneaded like bread dough.

Cut off about ¼ of the dough. Roll out on a floured board to a thickness of about ½". Cut the rolled dough into strips, ½" wide. Then cut strips into ½" pieces. Spread pieces apart and roll each piece over tines of a fork to make ridges or the traditional shell shape. If necessary, sprinkle pieces with flour or dip tines of the fork in flour to keep the dough from sticking. OR: press your thumb into the center of each piece to make an indentation. After the pieces are shaped, put them on cookie sheets which have been lined with waxed paper and separate the pieces to keep them from sticking together. Repeat the process until all the dough has been used (shaping the gnocchi is usually a family affair, as many hands make it fun rather than work). Gnocchi do not keep well, so they should be cooked as soon as they are made.

TO COOK: Fill a large pot with water and bring to a rolling boil. Add 1 Tbsp. salt and the gnocchi. Stir constantly until the water comes to a boil. Continue boiling until gnocchi rise to the top of the water and are cooked (about 10 minutes). Drain, cover with tomato sauce and mix gently. Pass extra sauce and grated Romano cheese to add as desired.

Serves 4 to 6.

CORN MEAL
(Polenta)

2 cups yellow corn meal
7 cups water
2 tsp. salt

Pour 5 cups cold water and the salt into a large pan (such as a soup kettle) and bring to a boil.

In a small bowl, thoroughly mix corn meal with 2 cups cold water. Add corn meal mixture to the boiling water, stirring constantly. Bring the mixture to a boil over high heat, stirring constantly. Cover and lower heat so the corn meal boils gently. Cook for about 30 minutes, stirring frequently, until the mixture is thick and smooth.

Using a soup ladle, pour the corn meal into dinner-size plates and spread to ½" thickness. Cover with tomato sauce and add grated Romano cheese to taste.

NOTE: For a tasty side dish, leftover corn meal, without sauce, can be cooled and refrigerated until firm. Cut the corn meal into squares and fry in hot oil until browned and crusty. Turn and brown on the other side. Serve hot, sprinkled with grated Romano cheese, if desired.

Serves 4.

NONNIE SAYS, "Tomato sauce made with sausage is traditionally served with polenta."

HOMEMADE PASTA
(Pasta Fatta in Casa)

2 large eggs
1½ to 2 cups flour

Put the flour on a large wooden board or a table. Make a well in the center of the flour and break eggs into the well. Using a fork, beat the eggs until well mixed. Add a little flour from the edge of the well and continue beating and adding flour until most of the flour is used. With your hands, work the remaining flour into the dough and knead until it is smooth and elastic (about 5 to 10 minutes).

Rub the dough with a little oil and let rest in a covered bowl for about ½ hour. Divide dough into two portions. Set one portion aside and cover with bowl. Roll out other portion on a lightly floured board. Roll from the center outward, turning the dough ¼ turn each time. Shape into a large, thin circle about 1/16" thick (thinner if you like). Repeat with other portion. Place the rolled out sheets of dough on a towel and let dry until they can be folded without sticking together (about 15 to 45 minutes, depending on the humidity). Do not dry too much, or they will crack.

When each sheet is ready, flour lightly and fold it very loosely over on itself until the entire sheet is folded into a roll about 2" wide (if dough is too sticky, sprinkle cornmeal on the sheet before folding; the cornmeal will fall out when dough is cut into strips).

Put folded dough on a large cutting board. Hold dough lightly with the fingers of one hand. Use a sharp knife to cut across the folded dough to make strips as wide or narrow as you like. Separate the cut pasta and dry on waxed paper.

TO COOK: Add pasta to boiling, salted water. Bring to a boil and cook until al dente (about 1 to 2 minutes). Drain, cover with tomato sauce and serve immediately. Pass grated cheese to add as desired.

Serves 2 to 3.

MANICOTTI

1 cup flour
1 cup water
1 egg

1½ lbs. ricotta
½ cup grated Romano cheese
½ lb. mozzarella, shredded
¼ cup chopped parsley
1 egg
5 to 6 cups tomato sauce

    Mix flour and water until smooth and then add the egg. Lightly oil a 6" frying pan and heat until oil is hot. Pour a spoonful of batter into the pan, spread around to cover the bottom of the pan with a light coating of the batter (similar to a crepe) and cook until batter is lightly browned on bottom. It is not necessary to turn the cooked shells over. Place shells on waxed paper to cool slightly.

    Combine ricotta and cheeses, parsley and egg. Mix well. Spoon some of the filling into the center of each shell and then fold over the edges, like a crepe, with the ends of the shell on top.

    Cover the bottom of a baking dish with a layer of warm tomato sauce. Place the filled manicotti on the sauce in a single layer. Cover with more sauce, sprinkle with additional grated Romano cheese, and bake for about 15 to 20 minutes at 350°. Pass any remaining sauce to add as desired.

Serves 4.

RICE SALAD
(Insalata Di Riso)

½ cup rice
¼ cup olive oil
2 Tbsp. white vinegar
1 Tbsp. finely chopped onion
2 Tbsp. chopped celery
¼ cup mozzarella cheese,
   cut in ¼" cubes
¼ cup chopped olives
1 hard boiled egg, sliced
3 olives, sliced

Cook rice until tender. While still hot, add oil and vinegar. Let stand until cool. Then add salt and pepper to taste and remaining ingredients, except the sliced egg and olives. Mix lightly.

Pour into a serving dish and garnish with the sliced egg and olives. Serve at room temperature or chilled.

Serves 4.

STUFFED TOMATOES
(Pomodori Ripiene)

6 medium-sized fresh tomatoes, ripe but firm
¼ cup oil
2 Tbsp. chopped celery leaves
1 Tbsp. chopped onion
⅛ tsp. minced garlic
½ cup grated Romano cheese
2 Tbsp. chopped parsley
½ cup rice, uncooked

Wash the tomatoes, cut off the top ¼" of each one and reserve. Scoop out the pulp and seeds and place in a bowl. Lightly salt the insides of the tomatoes and turn cut side down to drain.

Combine the remaining ingredients and stir well. Fill each tomato about ¾ full with the rice mixture. Cover with the reserved tops and place in a baking dish (do not crowd the tomatoes). Pour about ¼ cup of water into the bottom of the dish.

Bake tomatoes, uncovered, at 350° for about ½ hour. Remove tomatoes from oven, baste with juice in the pan, and cover pan with foil. Return tomatoes to the oven and bake another ½ hour, or until the rice is tender.

Serves 4 to 6.

CLAM SAUCE AND SPAGHETTI
(Spaghetti Con Vongole)

¾ cup olive oil
1¼ tsp. minced garlic
1 dozen clams, shucked, and cut into
   small pieces (Save liquid from clams)
2 Tbsp. chopped parsley
1 lb. spaghetti (or linguine)
Grated Romano cheese
Hot pepper (optional)

Pour oil into a deep pan. Add garlic and heat for about 10 to 20 seconds, until it just begins to turn light golden color. Add the clam juice immediately and bring to a boil. When the juice becomes foamy, lower the heat until the foaming subsides.

Add the clams and turn up the heat until the mixture comes to a boil. Stir in the parsley and remove from the heat immediately (the clams will become tough if they cook too long).

Cook the spaghetti in boiling, salted water until al dente. Drain, reserving about 1 cup of the cooking water to use if the spaghetti becomes too dry.

Pour clam sauce over the spaghetti. Mix well and serve immediately. Pass grated cheese and black and hot pepper to add as desired.

Serves 4 to 6.

NONNIE SAYS, "Clam sauce is also delicious with angel hair pasta, but you'll need more sauce."

MUSHROOM MARINARA SAUCE
(Salsa Di Funghi)

1 lb. mushrooms
3 to 4 Tbsp. oil
¼ tsp. minced garlic
1 Tbsp. chopped parsley
1 recipe marinara sauce
Grated Romano cheese

Heat oil in a large pan. Saute mushrooms over medium-high heat, stirring occasionally, for about 5 to 7 minutes. Add garlic and parsley. Season with salt and pepper to taste. Cook for another 2 to 3 minutes, stirring constantly.

Add mushrooms to marinara sauce and cook together for about ½ hour to blend flavors. Serve over freshly cooked pasta. Pass grated cheese to add as desired.

Serves 4 to 6.

TOMATO SAUCE
(Salsa Di Marinara)

¼ cup oil
¼ tsp. minced garlic
1 Tbsp. chopped parsley
1 28 oz. can crushed tomatoes

Heat oil, add garlic and parsley and saute for about 10 to 20 seconds, stirring constantly. Add crushed tomatoes and simmer, uncovered, for 10 to 15 minutes. Cover and simmer for another 15 to 20 minutes, stirring occasionally. Add a little water if the sauce becomes too thick. Season with salt and pepper to taste. Makes enough sauce for about ½ lb. pasta (depending on the type of pasta used).

Yields about 3 cups sauce.

NONNIE SAYS, "This sauce can be added to any tomato sauce if you run short or can be used as is for eggplant parmesan, baked macaroni or any other dish that requires a plain sauce."

SPAGHETTI WITH GARLIC AND OIL
(Spaghetti All' Aglio E Olio)

¾ cup olive oil
3 large cloves garlic, cut in halves
1 lb. spaghetti
Grated Romano cheese

Cook spaghetti in boiling, salted water until al dente. Drain spaghetti lightly, reserving about 1/2 cup of the cooking water.

While the spaghetti is cooking, heat oil in a medium saucepan. Add garlic and cook, stirring constantly, until garlic is light golden in color (do not cook too long, or it becomes very bitter). Remove garlic and discard. OR: Mince the garlic, add to the oil and cook only about 10 to 20 seconds. Leave the garlic in the oil for a nice flavor.

Remove oil from heat immediately and pour over cooked spaghetti. Add a little of the reserved cooking water if spaghetti is too dry. Serve at once. Pass grated cheese and black or hot red pepper to add as desired.

Serves 4.

TUNA FISH SAUCE AND SPAGHETTI

(Salsa Di Tonno Con Spaghetti)

¼ cup olive oil
2 Tbsp. chopped onion
2 Tbsp. chopped parsley
1 can (28 oz.) plum tomatoes
1 can (6½ oz.) tuna fish, packed in oil
1 lb. spaghetti
Grated Romano cheese

Heat oil, add onion and parsley and saute for a few minutes, until tender. Put tomatoes in a blender or chop finely and add to the onion mixture. Cook for about 1/2 hour, stirring occasionally. Add tuna and the oil in which it is packed and continue cooking for about 20 minutes.

Cook spaghetti in boiling, salted water until al dente. Drain, put in a bowl and cover with the sauce. Pass grated cheese to add as desired. Serve immediately.

Serves 4.

TOMATO MEAT SAUCE
(Ragu Di Carne)

1½ lbs. meat (meatballs, sausage,
 braciole, chunks of beef or pork,
 or any combination of these)
¼ cup oil
2 tsp. finely chopped onion
½ tsp. minced garlic
1 Tbsp. chopped fresh parsley
1 28 oz. can crushed tomatoes
1 tsp. salt
⅛ tsp. pepper
1 6 oz. can tomato paste
2 to 3 cans water

Heat oil in a large pan and brown the meat on all sides. When meat is browned, add chopped onions and fry until soft. Add garlic and parsley and fry for about 10 to 20 seconds, stirring constantly. Add crushed tomatoes and bring to a boil. Lower heat and simmer, uncovered, for about ½ hour.

Add tomato paste. Then fill the tomato paste can with water two or three times and stir the water into the sauce until well blended. Season with salt and pepper to taste. Cover and continue cooking for about 1½ hours, stirring occasionally.

Serve over cooked pasta. This sauce is enough for 1 to 1½ lbs. pasta, depending on the type of pasta used.

NOTE: Tomato sauce, with or without meat, freezes well.

Serves 6 to 8.

Chicken Meat & Seafood

BREADED CHICKEN BREASTS
(Petto Di Pollo Fritto)

1 lb. boneless chicken breasts, sliced ½" thick
1 Tbsp. chopped parsley
¼ tsp. minced garlic
1 Tbsp. grated Romano cheese
1 cup bread crumbs
2 eggs, beaten well
½ cup oil (approx.) for frying
Lemon wedges (optional)

Combine the parsley, garlic, cheese and bread crumbs.

Lightly salt the chicken and dip each piece in the bread crumb mixture (or substitute flour for the bread crumbs) and coat evenly.

Heat oil in a deep pan (there should be about 1" of oil). Dip each coated piece of chicken in beaten eggs and fry until golden brown.

Place the breasts on a wire rack in a baking pan. Bake at 325° for about 10 minutes to finish cooking (some of the oil will drain off at this time). Place chicken pieces on a warm platter and serve immediately, with lemon wedges, if desired.

Serves 4.

CHICKEN WITH PEPPERS
(Pollo E Peperoni)

3 lbs. chicken, cut up
¼ cup oil
3 to 4 large peppers, cut into
   strips about 1" wide

Heat oil in a large pan, add chicken and saute until browned on all sides. Add salt and pepper to taste and 1 to 2 Tbsp. water. Cover and continue cooking slowly, stirring occasionally, for about an hour or until tender and cooked through. Add 1 to 2 Tbsp. more water during the cooking if chicken starts to dry out.

Remove chicken from the pan and keep warm on a platter. Add peppers to the oil remaining in the pan and cook until firm but tender. Add salt to taste. Return chicken to pan and cook with the peppers for about 10 to 15 minutes.

Carefully lift out chicken and peppers and place on a platter. Add 2 to 3 Tbsp. water to drippings in the pan, boil for about a minute, and pour over the chicken and peppers.

Serves 4.

ROAST CHICKEN AND POTATOES
(Arrosto Di Pollo E Patate)

3 lbs. chicken, cut up
1 to 2 Tbsp. oil
4 large potatoes

Heat oven to 375°. Use the oil to grease a large roasting pan. Sprinkle the chicken with salt and pepper and place in the pan. Bake for about 45 minutes, basting occasionally, until chicken is browned and almost cooked.

Slice the potatoes as you would for French fries. Remove the chicken from the oven and add the potatoes to the oil in the pan (if necessary, add enough oil so the potatoes are all coated with oil). Place the chicken pieces on top of the potatoes.

Bake for about 30 minutes and then stir the potatoes carefully. Bake for about 20 minutes more, until chicken and potatoes are tender. Remove chicken from oven and keep warm on a platter. Turn oven up to 450° and bake potatoes for about 5 minutes more, until browned.

Serves 4.

SAUTEED CHICKEN BREASTS WITH WINE
(Petto Di Pollo Con Vino)

1 lb. boneless chicken breasts
3 Tbsp. oil
2 to 3 Tbsp. white wine
1 to 2 tsp. chopped parsley
¼ to ½ tsp. minced garlic

Heat oil in shallow pan. Saute chicken breasts on both sides until they begin to brown. Lower heat and add 1 to 2 Tbsp. water (or more) to keep chicken from drying out. Continue cooking for about 15 to 20 minutes. Then add salt and pepper to taste. Add minced garlic and parsley to the pan drippings and cook for about 10 to 20 seconds, stirring constantly, until garlic is lightly browned.

Add the wine and cook uncovered for about 1 to 2 minutes, stirring the juice constantly. Then cover and cook about 2 to 3 minutes more. Add a little more water or wine if the chicken becomes dry.

NOTE: This dish can be made ahead of time and reheated.

Serves 3 to 4.

MARINATED STEAK
(Bistecca Al Forno)

3 or 4 lbs. sirloin steak

Marinade:
¼ cup oil
2 Tbsp. wine vinegar
1 clove minced garlic
1 Tbsp. chopped parsley

Place steak in a baking dish. Mix marinade ingredients and pour over steak. Baste meat with marinade several times for 1 or 2 hours prior to cooking.

Broil steak, basting with marinade, for about 20 minutes per side, or until cooked as desired. Season with salt and pepper to taste and serve immediately.

Serves 6 to 8.

ROAST BEEF
(Arrosto Di Manzo)

3 to 3½ lbs. sirloin tip roast
1 to 2 Tbsp. olive oil
1 to 2 cloves garlic, slivered
2 to 3 sprigs of parsley
½ cup white or rose wine (optional)

With a sharp knife, make small slits at various spots on top of roast. Insert slivers of garlic and a piece of parsley into each slit. Rub the roast with oil on all sides.

Heat oven to 450°. Insert meat thermometer in roast. Place in a shallow pan and roast, uncovered, for 20 minutes. Lower heat to 325° and roast for about 1¼ to 1½ hours, until cooked as desired. Add optional wine (or ½ cup water) after the roast has been cooking for about an hour. Baste often with the wine and juices in the pan.

About 10 to 20 minutes before the roast is cooked, sprinkle with salt and pepper to taste.

Let the roast stand for 10 to 20 minutes after cooking for easier carving.

Serves 6 to 8.

THIN STEAK
(Bistecche Fritte)

> 1 lb. sirloin tip steak,
>   sliced ¼" thick
> 2 to 3 Tbsp. oil
> 2 to 3 Tbsp. water

Heat oil, add slices of steak and fry quickly. Brown the meat on each side and then add salt and pepper to taste.

Remove meat from pan and add the water. Boil about ½ minute, stirring constantly, until the water is reduced slightly. Pour over the meat and serve at once.

VARIATION: Add ⅛ tsp. minced garlic and 1 Tbsp. chopped parsley to the drippings in the pan just before adding the water. Thin steak can also be used to make a sandwich, with fried peppers and onions added for extra flavor.

Serves 4.

MEATBALLS
(Polpette Di Carne)

¾ lb. ground chuck
¾ lb. ground pork
¼ cup fresh bread crumbs
2 Tbsp. chopped parsley
¼ tsp. minced garlic
1 tsp. salt
2 eggs
2 Tbsp. grated Romano cheese
½ cup oil

Mix all the ingredients except oil. Wet palms of hands with water and then shape mixture into meatballs.

Heat oil in a large pan. Fry meatballs, turning frequently to brown on all sides. To use meatballs in tomato sauce, follow recipe for tomato meat sauce.

Yields 12 to 14 meatballs.

NONNIE SAYS, "Tomato sauce made with meatballs can be used over pasta or with crusty Italian bread or rolls for hot meatball sandwiches."

STUFFED PEPPERS
(Peperoni Ripieni)

4 to 5 large peppers
1 lb. ground beef
  (or half ground pork)
1 small egg, beaten
2 Tbsp. bread crumbs
¼ tsp. minced garlic
1 Tbsp. chopped fresh parsley
1 Tbsp. grated Romano cheese
1 tsp. salt
⅛ tsp. pepper
¼ cup oil for frying
1 16 oz. can crushed tomatoes (optional)
½ tsp. minced garlic

Wash peppers and remove core and seeds. Wipe outside with paper towels and sprinkle inside with salt.

Combine meat and all remaining ingredients except oil, tomatoes and ½ tsp. minced garlic. Mix well, divide into equal parts and fill peppers with the mixture.

Heat oil in a pan that has high sides. Fry peppers over medium heat, turning to brown all sides and ends evenly (this will take about ¾ to 1 hour). Serve at once.

OPTIONAL: Add the canned tomatoes after the peppers are browned. Season the tomatoes with salt and pepper and minced garlic. Continue cooking for about ½ hour, until sauce is thickened and flavors blend.

TO BAKE PEPPERS: After peppers are stuffed, place in a baking pan, pour the oil over the top of the peppers and bake at 325° for about 1 hour. If adding tomatoes, bake peppers for ½ hour, add tomatoes and bake for another ½ hour.

Serves 4.

STUFFED PEPPERS
(Peperoni Ripieni)

4 to 5 large peppers
1 lb. ground beef
   (or half ground pork)
1 small egg, beaten
2 Tbsp. bread crumbs
¼ tsp. minced garlic
1 Tbsp. chopped fresh parsley
1 Tbsp. grated Romano cheese
1 tsp. salt
⅛ tsp. pepper
¼ cup oil for frying
1 16 oz. can crushed tomatoes (optional)
½ tsp. minced garlic

Wash peppers and remove core and seeds. Wipe outside with paper towels and sprinkle inside with salt.

Combine meat and all remaining ingredients except oil, tomatoes and ½ tsp. minced garlic. Mix well, divide into equal parts and fill peppers with the mixture.

Heat oil in a pan that has high sides. Fry peppers over medium heat, turning to brown all sides and ends evenly (this will take about ¾ to 1 hour). Serve at once.

OPTIONAL: Add the canned tomatoes after the peppers are browned. Season the tomatoes with salt and pepper and minced garlic. Continue cooking for about ½ hour, until sauce is thickened and flavors blend.

TO BAKE PEPPERS: After peppers are stuffed, place in a baking pan, pour the oil over the top of the peppers and bake at 325° for about 1 hour. If adding tomatoes, bake peppers for ½ hour, add tomatoes and bake for another ½ hour.

Serves 4.

HOMEMADE SAUSAGE

(Salsiccia Casalinga)

1½ lb. ground pork
1 tsp. fennel seed (whole or ground)
1 Tbsp. oil
½ tsp. salt
¼ tsp. pepper

Mix pork, fennel seed, salt and pepper. Shape into patties or stuff into sausage casings.

Heat oil and saute sausage until browned on all sides. Cover and cook slowly, stirring occasionally, for about ½ hour, or until well cooked. Add 1 to 2 Tbsp. water, if needed, to keep sausage from drying out.

OPTIONAL SEASONINGS: 1 tsp. minced garlic
¼ tsp. hot pepper

NOTE: To grind your own pork, buy a lean pork butt. Trim pork off the bone before grinding. The pork bone can be added to tomato sauce for extra flavor.

Serves 4.

SAUSAGE AND PEPPERS
(Salsicce Con Peperoni)

1 lb. sausage
 (see homemade sausage recipe)
1 Tbsp. oil
4 large peppers, cored and
 cut into 1" strips
¼ tsp. minced garlic
¼ cup oil

Heat oil and saute sausage until browned on all sides. Cover and cook slowly, stirring occasionally, for about ½ hour, until sausage is well cooked. Remove to platter and keep warm.

Heat ¼ cup oil, add minced garlic, and saute for about 10 to 20 seconds. Add about half the peppers and fry over medium heat, stirring frequently, until firm but tender. Using a slotted spoon, remove cooked peppers (but not the oil) and keep warm with the sausage.

Add the rest of the peppers to the pan and cook until firm but tender. Return the sausage and reserved peppers to the pan and season with salt and pepper to taste. Cook until sausage and peppers are heated through and flavors blend.

Serves 3 to 4.

VEAL PARMESAN
(Vitello Parmigiana)

1 lb. veal, sliced ¼" thick
2 eggs, beaten
1 cup bread crumbs
¼ cup chopped parsley
2 Tbsp. grated Romano or
    Parmesan cheese
½ to ¾ cup oil for frying
2 cups tomato sauce
½ lb. mozzarella cheese,
    grated or sliced

Mix bread crumbs, parsley and Romano cheese. Lightly salt veal slices. Dip slices in beaten eggs and then in bread crumb mixture. Fry in hot oil until golden brown on both sides.

Spread a thin layer of sauce on bottom of a baking pan. Arrange cooked veal slices on the sauce and top each slice with more sauce. Sprinkle with additional grated Romano or Parmesan cheese, if desired.

Bake at 325° for about 20 minutes. Top each slice of veal with mozzarella cheese and bake an additional 5 minutes, or until cheese melts.

Serves 4.

VEAL AND PEPPERS
(Vitello E Peperoni)

    4 to 5 veal chops or
    1½ pounds stew veal
    ¼ cup oil
    4 peppers, cut into ½ inch strips
    ¼ tsp. minced garlic
    1 tsp. minced parsley
    3 to 4 Tbsp. wine (optional)

    Heat oil in a large pan. Add veal and brown on all sides. Add 1 to 2 Tbsp. water, cover and cook slowly, stirring occasionally, adding more water as needed. Cook until veal is tender and well cooked (about 45 minutes). Season with salt and pepper to taste.

    Add peppers and cook, uncovered, until peppers are tender but firm. Add garlic and parsley and fry for about 10 to 20 seconds, stirring constantly. Add more salt, if needed, and 3 to 4 Tbsp. water (or wine) and cook a few more minutes, stirring occasionally, until flavors are blended.

Serves 4.

VEAL STEW
(Vitello Stufato)

1½ pounds stew veal
¼ cup oil
1½ cups canned crushed tomatoes
4 medium potatoes, cubed
4 peppers, cut into ½" strips
1 medium onion, sliced

Heat oil in a large pan. Add veal and brown on all sides. Then add 1 to 2 Tbsp. water, cover and cook over low heat, stirring occasionally. Continue to add water, 1 to 2 Tbsp. at a time, if necessary, to keep meat from sticking. Cook for about 1 hour, until veal is tender. Season with salt and pepper to taste. Add tomatoes and cook 10 to 15 minutes, uncovered.

Add cubed potatoes and onion and cook about 10 minutes, covered. Add peppers and cook uncovered for another 10 to 15 minutes. Season with more salt if desired. Add water (or white wine) if sauce becomes too thick.

Serves 4 to 6.

LIVER AND ONIONS
(Fegato E Cepolle)

10 medium onions, sliced ¼" thick
6 Tbsp. oil
1 lb. chicken livers,
　　cut into 1" cubes
2 to 3 Tbsp. water

    Heat oil in a large pan. Add onions and saute, stirring often, until soft. Remove onions and keep warm on a platter. Cook liver in remaining oil on medium-high heat, stirring frequently, until browned on all sides. Add onions to liver in pan and cook together for about 3 to 4 minutes, until flavors blend. Season with salt and pepper to taste.

    Using a slotted spoon, lift liver and onions from pan and place on a serving plate. Add 2 to 3 Tbsp. water to oil and drippings in pan and bring to boil, stirring constantly. Pour over liver and onions and serve immediately.

Serves 4 generously.

BAKED FISH
(Pesce Al Forno)

1 lb. fresh or frozen fish fillets
2 Tbsp. oil
Juice of ½ lemon
1 Tbsp. chopped parsley
1 clove garlic, sliced
½ cup bread crumbs (optional)
¼ cup white wine

Place fish in a lightly oiled shallow pan. Pour oil and lemon juice over the fish and then sprinkle with chopped parsley and garlic. Marinate for ½ to 1 hour, basting frequently.

Just before baking, sprinkle each fillet with bread crumbs, if desired.

Bake at 400° for 10 to 15 minutes, until almost cooked. Remove from oven and pour wine over the fish. Bake for about 5 to 10 minutes more. Watch closely so the fish does not overcook. Fish is cooked when it flakes easily with a fork.

Serves 4.

FRIED SMELTS
(Pesce Fritti)

1 lb. fresh or frozen smelts
½ to ¾ cup flour
1 cup oil (approximately)

Cut off heads, fins, and tails of smelts (or leave the tails attached to hold onto while eating!). Use scissors to slit the underside of the smelts and remove insides. Wash smelts thoroughly and drain well.

Salt the smelts lightly just before frying. Put enough oil in a deep pan so that the oil is about 1" deep. Dip the salted smelts in flour to coat (or shake in a paper bag) and fry until golden brown. Do not overcook or the smelts will dry out. Serve warm.

NOTE: Fresh smelts are available in March in the Northeastern states, but available frozen any time.

Serves 3 to 4.

SALMON CROQUETTES
(Crocchetti Di Salmone)

1 can salmon, drained
1 Tbsp. finely chopped onion
1 egg, beaten
½ cup bread crumbs
2 Tbsp. oil
1 egg, beaten,
    for coating croquettes

Remove skin and bones from salmon. Mix salmon, onion, egg and add salt and pepper to taste. Shape into patties.

Dip patties in bread crumbs and then into beaten egg. Heat oil in frying pan and fry patties until golden on each side.

Yields 5 to 6 patties.

SCALLOPS
(Smerlo)

2 lbs. scallops ("calico" or small)
3 to 4 Tbsp. oil
½ tsp. minced garlic
1 Tbsp. chopped parsley
3 to 4 Tbsp. white wine (optional)

Heat oil in a frying pan, add scallops and fry on medium-high heat for about 3 minutes. Add garlic, parsley and salt and pepper to taste. Cook, stirring constantly, for about 1 minute more. Add wine, if desired, and cook an additional 30 seconds. Do not overcook scallops or they will become tough. Serve at once.

VARIATION: Scallops can also be broiled. To broil, mix scallops, oil and seasonings well. Place on a broiling pan and broil for 2 to 3 minutes, or until just cooked.

Serves 4 to 6.

Vegetables

ARTICHOKES WITH OIL AND OREGANO
(Carciofi All' Olio E Oregano)

4 medium artichokes, including stems
¼ tsp. salt
⅛ tsp. pepper
¼ tsp. oregano
1 large clove garlic, cut into 12 slivers
2 tsp. bread crumbs (optional)
1 tsp. grated Romano cheese (optional)
1 tsp. chopped parsley (optional)
¼ cup oil

Wash artichokes. Cut off stems flush with base, peel and set aside. Break off leaves, starting from bottom and working towards top, to remove tough outer leaves. Cut across top of artichoke to remove sharp tips and make top flat. Spread leaves apart slightly and sprinkle each artichoke with salt and pepper and oregano. Insert 2 or 3 slivers of garlic into the leaves of each artichoke and add optional bread crumbs, grated cheese and parsley.

Put about 1" of water in a pan that will hold all the artichokes upright. Add the artichokes and stems and pour a tablespoon of oil over the top of each artichoke. Cover the pan and bring to a boil.

Simmer gently for 35 to 45 minutes, basting frequently, until base of artichokes can be pierced easily with a fork (add more water if needed).

Serves 4.

NONNIE SAYS, "Artichokes are delicious served hot, but are very good served at room temperature too."

ASPARAGUS WITH OIL AND GARLIC
(Asparagi A Aglio E Olio)

1½ lbs. fresh asparagus
2 cups water
3 Tbsp. oil
⅛ tsp. minced garlic
Lemon wedges (optional)

Break or cut off tough lower stem of asparagus. Bring water to boil and add asparagus. Cook until fork tender, about 5 to 10 minutes, depending on size of the asparagus. Use a slotted spoon to carefully remove asparagus from water.

Heat oil, add minced garlic, and saute for about 10 to 20 seconds, stirring constantly. Then add asparagus and cook over medium heat, stirring carefully for about 2 to 3 minutes. Season with salt and pepper to taste.

VARIATION: While the asparagus is still warm, place on serving platter, season with salt and pepper to taste, and add garlic. Drizzle oil over the spears. Serve with lemon wedges, if desired.

Serves 4.

ASPARAGUS WITH OIL AND GARLIC
(Asparagi A Aglio E Olio)

1½ lbs. fresh asparagus
2 cups water
3 Tbsp. oil
⅛ tsp. minced garlic
Lemon wedges (optional)

Break or cut off tough lower stem of asparagus. Bring water to boil and add asparagus. Cook until fork tender, about 5 to 10 minutes, depending on size of the asparagus. Use a slotted spoon to carefully remove asparagus from water.

Heat oil, add minced garlic, and saute for about 10 to 20 seconds, stirring constantly. Then add asparagus and cook over medium heat, stirring carefully for about 2 to 3 minutes. Season with salt and pepper to taste.

VARIATION: While the asparagus is still warm, place on serving platter, season with salt and pepper to taste, and add garlic. Drizzle oil over the spears. Serve with lemon wedges, if desired.

Serves 4.

BAKED ZUCCHINI
(Zucchini Al Forno)

1 large zucchini
1½ cups bread crumbs (approximately)
¼ cup grated Romano cheese
½ cup oil
½ lb. mozzarella (optional)

Wash, dry and peel zucchini. Cut crosswise into sections about 5" long. Cut each section into lengthwise slices ½" thick by slicing until you come to the seeds. Turn the section and continue slicing until only the inside seed section is left. Discard the seed section.

Mix bread crumbs with grated cheese. Lightly salt the sliced zucchini. Dip each slice in oil and then in seasoned bread crumbs.

Place the slices on a lightly oiled baking sheet and bake for 20 minutes at 400°. It is not necessary to turn the slices over.

OPTIONAL: Slice or shred the mozzarella and sprinkle on top of each slice. Continue baking for about 5 minutes, or until the cheese melts.

Serves 6.

NONNIE SAYS, "This is a good way to use up those very large zucchini you get in the summer."

BAKED STUFFED MUSHROOMS
(Funghi Ripieni Al Forno)

1 lb. mushrooms
1 cup bread crumbs (approx.)
3 Tbsp. oil
1 Tbsp. grated Romano cheese
¼ tsp. minced garlic
1 Tbsp. chopped parsley

Carefully wash and dry the mushrooms and break off the stems. Chop about ½ cup of the mushroom stems and mix with the remaining ingredients. (Any extra stems can be baked with the caps or saved for use later.)

Salt the inside of the mushroom caps and fill with stuffing (the stuffing shrinks when baked, so pack firmly).

Place stuffed caps in lightly oiled baking pan. Bake, uncovered, at 400° for about 45 minutes. After 20 minutes, baste with the juice in the pan (if there isn't enough juice, add 1 to 2 Tbsp. water). Baste again when almost cooked. Serve warm.

NOTE: Leftover stuffing can be frozen or added to meatballs for a nice flavor.

Serves 4.

BAKED STUFFED MUSHROOMS
(Funghi Ripieni Al Forno)

1 lb. mushrooms
1 cup bread crumbs (approx.)
3 Tbsp. oil
1 Tbsp. grated Romano cheese
¼ tsp. minced garlic
1 Tbsp. chopped parsley

Carefully wash and dry the mushrooms and break off the stems. Chop about ½ cup of the mushroom stems and mix with the remaining ingredients. (Any extra stems can be baked with the caps or saved for use later.)

Salt the inside of the mushroom caps and fill with stuffing (the stuffing shrinks when baked, so pack firmly).

Place stuffed caps in lightly oiled baking pan. Bake, uncovered, at 400° for about 45 minutes. After 20 minutes, baste with the juice in the pan (if there isn't enough juice, add 1 to 2 Tbsp. water). Baste again when almost cooked. Serve warm.

NOTE: Leftover stuffing can be frozen or added to meatballs for a nice flavor.

Serves 4.

BEETS WITH FRESH HERBS
(Barbabietola All' Olio)

4 cups fresh beets,
   cooked with skins on
¼ cup oil
3 to 4 chopped fresh basil leaves
½ tsp. chopped fresh oregano
   (OR ½ tsp. dried basil and
     ¼ tsp. dried oregano)
1 Tbsp. chopped fresh parsley
½ tsp. minced garlic
1 Tbsp. vinegar (optional)

Peel and slice the beets as soon as they are cooked. Add remaining ingredients while the beets are still warm and mix well. Prepare at least one-half hour before serving to allow flavors to blend.

Serves 4 to 6.

NONNIE SAYS, "Fresh beets are delicious served warm, but they are also good after they are chilled and the seasonings blend."

CABBAGE WITH TOMATOES
(Cavoli Con Pomodoro)

1 head cabbage (about 2 lbs.)
½ to ¾ cup water
1¼ cups crushed tomatoes
¼ cup oil
½ tsp. minced garlic

Clean cabbage and cut into slices about ½" thick. Heat oil in a large pan. Add minced garlic and saute for about 10 to 20 seconds. Add cabbage and water, cover and cook for about ½ hour, stirring occasionally. Add crushed tomatoes, cover and cook for another ½ hour, until cabbage is firm but tender. Season with salt add pepper to taste.

Serves 6 to 8.

NONNIE SAYS, "Cabbage is also delicious cooked this way, but without the tomatoes."

CAULIFLOWER WITH PARSLEY
(Cavolfiori All' Prezzemolo)

1 medium head cauliflower,
   broken into florets
2 cups water
¼ cup oil
¼ tsp. minced garlic
1 Tbsp. chopped parsley

Bring water to a boil, add cauliflower and cook until fork tender (about 5 to 10 minutes). Remove cauliflower from water.

Heat oil, saute garlic for about 10 to 20 seconds, stirring constantly. Add cauliflower and parsley and continue cooking for about 5 minutes. Season with salt and pepper to taste.

Serves 4 to 6.

FRIED EGGPLANT
(Melanzane Fritte)

2 medium size eggplants
2 eggs, beaten
½ cup flour (more if needed)
½ to ¾ cup oil for frying
Lemon wedges (optional)

Peel eggplants and cut in slices ¼" thick. Salt on both sides and place in dish with another dish on top. Weight the dish with an iron or any heavy object and let eggplant slices drain for at least 1 hour. Pour off drained liquid 2 to 3 times during the hour.

After the eggplant slices have drained, coat each slice with flour on both sides, then dip in beaten eggs, and fry until golden brown on both sides.

NOTE: Eggplant prepared this way can be used for eggplant parmesan.

Serves 6 to 8.

EGGPLANT PARMESAN
(Melanzane Alla Parmigiana)

2 medium eggplants,
  (follow recipe for Fried Eggplant)
2 cups tomato sauce (approximately)
½ lb. mozzarella cheese, sliced or shredded
¼ to ½ cup grated Romano or Parmesan cheese

Spread a thin layer of tomato sauce in a 9 x 13" baking dish. Arrange eggplant slices to cover bottom of dish. Cover with a layer of tomato sauce, sprinkle with grated cheese and then the sliced or shredded mozzarella cheese. Add another layer of eggplant, tomato sauce and cheeses until all the eggplant slices are used. Top with tomato sauce, then sprinkle with Romano and mozzarella cheeses.

Cover with foil and bake at 350° for 30 minutes. Uncover and bake for another 10 to 15 minutes.

Serves 4 to 6.

EGGS WITH TOMATOES
(Uova Con Pomodori)

1 Tbsp. oil
½ cup canned crushed tomatoes
1 small onion, chopped (optional)
3 or 4 eggs, lightly beaten

Heat oil in frying pan, add crushed tomatoes and optional onion (or cook the onions briefly and then add tomatoes). Cook over medium heat, stirring frequently, for about 10 minutes.

Add beaten eggs and stir constantly until cooked to desired consistency, similar to scrambled eggs. Season with salt and pepper to taste.

Serves 2.

FRIED PEPPERS
(Peperoni Fritti)

4 large peppers
¼ cup oil
1 clove garlic, quartered

Wash peppers, remove core and cut into 1" strips. Heat oil in frying pan or dutch oven. Add garlic, brown lightly, and then remove garlic and discard.

Add about half the peppers to oil and fry on medium heat, stirring frequently, until firm but tender. Using a slotted spoon, remove cooked peppers (but not the oil) from pan and keep warm in a bowl.

Add the rest of the peppers to oil in the pan and cook until firm but tender. Return the reserved peppers to the pan, season with salt and pepper to taste, and cook until all peppers are seasoned and heated through.

Serves 4.

NONNIE SAYS, "Garlic can also be minced and added shortly before peppers have finished cooking. This gives the peppers a nice flavor, and you don't have to remove the garlic."

FRIED ZUCCHINI BLOSSOMS
(Fioro Di Zucchini Fritti)

10 zucchini blossoms
1 to 2 Tbsp. flour
1 egg
½ cup (or more) oil for frying

Beat egg and add flour. OR: Beat the egg and put flour on a sheet of waxed paper. Sprinkle flour or egg mixture with salt and pepper.

Pour oil into a small frying pan to a depth of 1". Heat oil until hot enough for frying.

Remove center from squash blossoms. Dip in egg mixture (or dip in flour and then in egg) and fry until golden. Serve at once.

Serves 4.

MARINATED EGGPLANT
(Melanzane Marinate)

1 large eggplant
1½ cups water
½ cup white vinegar
1 clove garlic, slivered
¼ tsp. oregano
¼ tsp. crushed red pepper (optional)
½ to ¾ cup oil
1 tsp. salt

Wash eggplant, peel, and cut into slices ¼" thick. Then cut the slices into strips ¼" wide.

Bring water and vinegar to a boil in a large pan. Add eggplant strips and more water if necessary to cover the eggplant. Boil for 2 minutes. Drain eggplant and then squeeze to remove all the water. Place in a bowl and season with salt, garlic, oregano, hot pepper and oil. Mix well.

Place the eggplant strips in a wide-mouth jar (a one quart size is usually enough for one large eggplant). Add eggplant strips in layers, pushing strips down with your hand or a wooden spoon to pack firmly. When the jar is filled, add enough additional oil, if necessary, to cover the strips. Cover the jar and refrigerate. Eggplant prepared this way will keep for months, and the flavor improves with age.

To serve: use in an antipasto or as a sandwich filling with crusty Italian bread.

Yields 1 quart.

MIXED DEEP FRIED VEGETABLES
(Fritto Misto Di Verdura)

Use only fresh vegetables,
  cleaned and washed

6 to 8 asparagus spears
1 cup whole mushrooms
1 cup cauliflower florets
1 cup broccoli florets
1 artichoke, cut into eighths, with outer
  leaves and inside "choke" removed
2 to 3 eggs, beaten
¾ to 1 cup flour
1 cup oil for frying (more if needed)
1 or 2 lemons, cut into wedges

    Cook each type of vegetable separately (except mushrooms) in boiling water until just firm. Drain and salt lightly. Dip each piece of vegetable in flour to coat evenly and then dip into beaten eggs.

    Heat oil in a small, deep pan. Fry coated vegetables until golden in color. Drain on paper towels.

    Serve with lemon wedges, if desired.

NOTE: Bread crumbs can be used instead of flour.

Serves 4 to 6.

MUSHROOMS WITH GARLIC AND PARSLEY

(Funghi Al Olio)

1 lb. mushrooms
3 to 4 Tbsp. oil
¼ tsp. minced garlic
1 Tbsp. chopped parsley

Wash mushrooms and dry with paper towels. Cut into quarters or slices.

Heat oil in a large frying pan. Add mushrooms and fry over medium-high heat, stirring frequently, for about 5 to 10 minutes or until cooked. Add minced garlic, parsley and salt and pepper to taste. Fry for a few more minutes, until seasonings blend and mushrooms are cooked to taste.

Serves 4.

OVEN FRIED POTATOES
(Patate Al Forno)

4 medium potatoes
½ cup oil

Wash and peel potatoes. Cut the potatoes as you would for French fries. Put the potatoes in a large shallow baking pan with 2" sides (make only one layer of potatoes). Add the oil and stir until potatoes are coated. Add salt and pepper to taste.

Bake at 400° to 425°. After 15 minutes, stir potatoes carefully with a flat spatula. Bake for another 30 to 45 minutes, until potatoes are brown and crisp. Potatoes can be placed under the broiler to finish browning, but watch carefully so they don't burn.

Serves 4.

RADISHES AND OIL
(Ravanelli All' Olio)

1 bunch radishes
2 Tbsp. oil
½ tsp. salt
¼ tsp. pepper

Wash radishes and cut in half, leaving stems and root ends on for a "handle."

Pour oil into a shallow dish; add salt and pepper and mix well.

To eat: Dip each radish half into the oil mixture.

Serves 2.

RAPI
(Broccoli Di Rapi)

2 lbs. rapi (NOT rapini; see below)
(Fresh rapi is available from
November to March only)
¼ cup oil

Clean and wash the rapi and drain lightly. Put oil and rapi in large pan. Cook, covered, over medium heat, stirring often to be sure the rapi does not stick to the pan. Add a little more water, if necessary. Cook until tender and still bright green (about 10 minutes).

Add salt to taste and serve hot.

Serves 4.

NONNIE SAYS, "These are Grandpa's favorite greens, served freshly cooked, with crusty Italian bread to dip in the juice."

RAPINI

Rapini is a different variety of vegetable and requires a different type of cooking. To cook rapini, follow directions for cooking swiss chard.

ROAST PEPPERS
(Peperoni Arrostiti)

6 green or red peppers with thick skins
¼ cup oil
1 to 2 Tbsp. chopped parsley
1 Tbsp. chopped fresh basil
1 clove garlic, sliced

Wash and dry the peppers. Place whole peppers on a large, flat baking sheet (with sides). Roast at 450° or under broiler, turning about every 5 minutes, until skins are blistered and loose.

****Place the peppers in a covered dish or kettle for about 10 minutes to help loosen the skins. Carefully peel off skins. Remove core and seeds, and cut peppers into strips about 1" wide.

Place strips of peppers in a bowl, add oil, parsley, basil, garlic and salt and pepper to taste. Mix well and let stand at room temperature for about an hour. Remove garlic slices before serving. Serve at room temperature.

ALTERNATE ROASTING METHOD: After washing and drying peppers, remove core and seeds. Cut peppers into thirds and place on pan, skin side up, and roast at 450° or under broiler until skins are blistered and loose. Continue from **** above.

NOTE: Roast peppers freeze very well, as long as you DO NOT ADD ANY SEASONING BEFORE FREEZING. Add the seasoning AFTER the peppers have thawed.

Serves 4.

SAUTEED ESCAROLE OR ENDIVE
(Escarola Al Olio)

8 cups escarole or endive
½ to 1 cup water for pressure cooker
   or 3 cups water for regular pan
¼ cup oil
¼ tsp. chopped garlic

TO COOK IN PRESSURE COOKER: Put escarole or endive and water in pressure cooker. Cook under pressure for 1 to 1½ minutes. Let pressure drop immediately by running cold water over pressure cooker.

TO COOK IN A REGULAR PAN: Bring water to a boil in a large kettle. Add escarole or endive. Cover pan and bring to a boil, stirring once or twice. Boil, covered, for 10 to 15 minutes, until tender.

TO SEASON ESCAROLE OR ENDIVE, COOKED BY EITHER METHOD:

Drain greens well. Pour oil in a pan, add garlic and cooked escarole or endive and saute for 5 to 10 minutes, stirring frequently. Season with salt and pepper to taste.

Serves 4.

SAUTEED ONIONS
(Cipolle Stufate)

4 large onions
3 Tbsp. oil
2 to 3 Tbsp. white vinegar
½ to 1 tsp. sugar
1 bay leaf (optional)

Peel onions and slice into rings ¼" thick. Saute in oil, stirring until translucent and well cooked.

Add the vinegar, sugar, salt to taste and bay leaf, if desired. Cook a few minutes more, until flavors are blended. Remove bay leaf before serving.

Serves 4.

STRING BEANS WITH OIL AND GARLIC

(Fagiolini All' Olio)

1 lb. fresh string beans
2 cups water
3 Tbsp. oil
¼ tsp. minced garlic

Remove tips from ends of string beans, wash, and break in half or leave whole. Bring the water to a boil. Add the string beans and cook for about 10 minutes, or until tender (or cook for 1½ min. in a pressure cooker). Gently lift string beans from water.

In another pan, heat oil, add garlic and saute for about 10 to 20 seconds, stirring constantly. Add string beans and saute for about 5 minutes. Season with salt and pepper to taste.

Serves 4 to 6.

STRING BEAN SALAD
(Fagiolini All' Insalata)

1 lb. fresh string beans
½ tsp. salt
1 Tbsp. chopped fresh parsley
1 tsp. chopped fresh basil
1 tsp. chopped fresh oregano
⅛ tsp. minced garlic
3 Tbsp. olive oil
2 Tbsp. wine vinegar

Wash and trim the string beans. Cook until tender. While the string beans are still warm, add the remaining ingredients in the order given. Mix lightly and let stand for about ½ hour, stirring occasionally to blend flavors. Serve warm or at room temperature.

NOTE: You may substitute dried herbs for fresh, but use less of each.

Serves 4.

STUFFED EGGPLANT
(Melanzane Ripiene)

1 large eggplant
2 Tbsp. oil
¼ tsp. minced garlic
1 Tbsp. chopped onion
½ lb. ground chuck
½ lb. ground pork
1 Tbsp. grated Romano cheese
1 Tbsp. chopped parsley or celery leaves
1 tsp. salt
⅛ tsp. black pepper
¼ cup bread crumbs (optional)

Tomato mixture:
1 cup tomato puree or crushed tomatoes
¼ tsp. salt
1 Tbsp. oil
pepper to taste

Wash eggplant, cut in half lengthwise and scoop out inside, leaving a shell about ½" all the way around. Salt inside of eggplant and turn cut side down to drain. Chop scooped-out inside of eggplant, sprinkle with salt, and set aside to drain.

Heat oil in a medium pan. Add onion and saute until tender. Add minced garlic and cook for about 10 to 20 seconds. Add meat, chopped eggplant and remaining ingredients, except for bread crumbs and tomato mixture. Cook for about 5 to 10 minutes, until meat is lightly browned.

Place half the mixture in each eggplant half, mounding it slightly on top (the mixture will shrink as it bakes). Combine ingredients for tomato mixture and spoon over stuffing. Cover with foil and bake at 350° for about 40 minutes. Uncover, top with bread crumbs if desired, and bake for an additional 15 to 20 minutes. To serve, cut each half of the stuffed eggplant in half or quarters.

VARIATION: Use a large zucchini in place of the eggplant.

Serves 4 to 6.

SAUTEED ZUCCHINI
(Zucchini All' Olio)

2 to 3 medium size zucchini
   (about 6 cups sliced)
¼ cup oil

Wash zucchini, cut in half lengthwise (or leave whole if zucchini are small), and cut into slices about ¼" thick.

Heat oil in a pan that has high sides. Add zucchini and cook over medium heat until tender (about 20 minutes). Stir frequently with a metal or plastic spatula, trying not to break up the slices. Season with salt and pepper to taste.

Serves 4.

ZUCCHINI, PEPPERS, ONIONS AND TOMATOES
(Zucchini, Peperoni, Cepolle E Pomodori)

3 to 4 fresh tomatoes, cut into sections
  or 1½ cups canned crushed tomatoes
¼ cup oil
1 large zucchini, cut in half lengthwise
  and sliced ¼" to ½" thick
2 peppers, cut into 1" strips
2 medium sized onions, sliced ½" thick

Heat oil and add fresh or canned tomatoes. Cook for 5 to 10 minutes. Add zucchini, peppers, and onions, stirring well to mix. Cover and simmer for ½ to ¾ hour, until vegetables are firm but tender. OR: cook each type of vegetable separately, using the same pan and adding a little more oil if needed before cooking the next vegetable. Then add the cooked vegetables to the tomatoes and simmer until flavors are blended, about 10 to 15 minutes. Season with salt and pepper to taste.

Serves 4.

NONNIE SAYS, "This dish is especially good with fresh, crusty Italian bread."

Salads

APPETIZER SALAD
(Antipasto)

Line a large plate or platter with lettuce leaves. Arrange attractively on the platter:

Thinly sliced: salami
cappocolla
pepperoni
prosciutto

mozzarella and provolone cheese

green and black olives

pepperoncini
marinated artichoke hearts
marinated eggplant strips
roast peppers
anchovies

fennel (finocchio)

Refrigerate until ready to serve.

Antipasto can be made with any selection of the above ingredients. The amounts used depend upon individual tastes and the number of people to be served.

ANCHOVY SALAD
(Insalata Con Acciuge)

1 2 oz. can anchovies, flat or rolled
1 tsp. minced garlic
2 Tbsp. wine vinegar
¼ cup oil
¼ tsp. salt

1 lb. endive or escarole, washed and
    cut into bite sized pieces

Drain oil from the anchovies and reserve. Mince garlic and spread on top of anchovies, then chop both together until the mixture resembles a paste.

Measure reserved oil from anchovies and add more if necessary to make ¼ cup. Add wine vinegar, salt, and anchovies. Stir until blended completely. Pour over the salad greens and toss until the greens are coated with the dressing.

Serves 4 to 6.

ANCHOVY SALAD
(Insalata Con Acciuge)

1 2 oz. can anchovies, flat or rolled
1 tsp. minced garlic
2 Tbsp. wine vinegar
¼ cup oil
¼ tsp. salt

1 lb. endive or escarole, washed and
   cut into bite sized pieces

Drain oil from the anchovies and reserve. Mince garlic and spread on top of anchovies, then chop both together until the mixture resembles a paste.

Measure reserved oil from anchovies and add more if necessary to make ¼ cup. Add wine vinegar, salt, and anchovies. Stir until blended completely. Pour over the salad greens and toss until the greens are coated with the dressing.

Serves 4 to 6.

ANCHOVY SALAD
(Insalata Con Acciuge)

1 2 oz. can anchovies, flat or rolled
1 tsp. minced garlic
2 Tbsp. wine vinegar
¼ cup oil
¼ tsp. salt

1 lb. endive or escarole, washed and
 cut into bite sized pieces

Drain oil from the anchovies and reserve. Mince garlic and spread on top of anchovies, then chop both together until the mixture resembles a paste.

Measure reserved oil from anchovies and add more if necessary to make ¼ cup. Add wine vinegar, salt, and anchovies. Stir until blended completely. Pour over the salad greens and toss until the greens are coated with the dressing.

Serves 4 to 6.

FRESH TOMATO SALAD
(Insalata Di Pomodori)

4 medium sized tomatoes, ripe but firm
2 to 3 Tbsp. oil
1 tsp. wine vinegar (optional)
3 to 4 fresh basil leaves, coarsely chopped
Salt and pepper to taste

Cut tomatoes into wedges. Add oil and seasoning and stir gently. Serve immediately.

OPTIONAL: Sliced cucumbers can be added to the tomatoes. Wine vinegar (1 to 2 tsp.) may also be added for flavor.

NOTE: If tomatoes are very ripe and watery, allow to drain for a few minutes after cutting. Pour off water and then prepare as above.

Serves 4.

LETTUCE SALAD
(Insalata)

1 lb. or 1 large head of
    romaine
    escarole
    endive
    or a mixture of all three

4 to 6 leaves fresh arugula or roquette (optional)

3 to 4 Tbsp. olive oil
2 to 3 Tbsp. wine vinegar*

Optional: Sliced tomatoes, cucumbers, carrots, celery, onions.

Wash lettuce and tear into bite-sized pieces. Add arugula or roquette and other vegetables, if desired.

Just before serving, add oil and vinegar and salt to taste. Mix to coat greens.

Serves 4 to 6.

*Can be made by combining equal parts of white vinegar and any dark, red wine. A clove of garlic can be added for extra flavor.

ORANGE SALAD
(Orangi Insalata)

4 oranges, peeled
3 to 4 Tbsp. oil
Italian bread (optional)

Cut oranges into bite-sized chunks. Season with oil and add salt and pepper to taste. Mix well and allow to stand for about ½ hour.

Serve at room temperature, with Italian bread to dip in the juice.

Serves 4.

POTATO SALAD WITH STRING BEANS AND TOMATOES
(Insalata Di Patate E Fagiolini)

4 medium sized potatoes, boiled whole
¼ cup oil
½ tsp. salt
¼ tsp. pepper
¼ tsp. oregano
2 Tbsp. wine vinegar (optional)
1 lb. fresh string beans
1 Tbsp. oil
¼ tsp. minced garlic
1 ripe medium sized tomato, cut into wedges

Boil potatoes until tender but firm. Peel and slice ¼" thick. Season with ¼ cup oil, salt and pepper to taste, oregano and wine vinegar.

Remove tips from ends of string beans, wash, and break in half. Cook until tender but firm. While warm, season with 1 Tbsp. oil, salt and pepper and garlic.

Place seasoned potatoes in the center of a serving plate. Arrange seasoned string beans around the edge of the potatoes in a ring shape. Just before serving, garnish with fresh tomato wedges.

Serves 4.

POTATO SALAD, ITALIAN STYLE
(Patate Insalata)

4 medium potatoes,
    peeled and cut into ¾" cubes
¼ cup oil
½ tsp. salt
¼ tsp. oregano
1 Tbsp. wine vinegar (optional)

Boil potatoes until tender but firm (about 8 to 10 minutes). Drain, saving a little of the cooking water to use later if needed.

Place potatoes in a bowl and add remaining ingredients. Stir lightly (so potatoes do not break up) until blended. Add a bit of the reserved water if potatoes are too dry. Serve warm.

Serves 4.

Sweets & Fruits

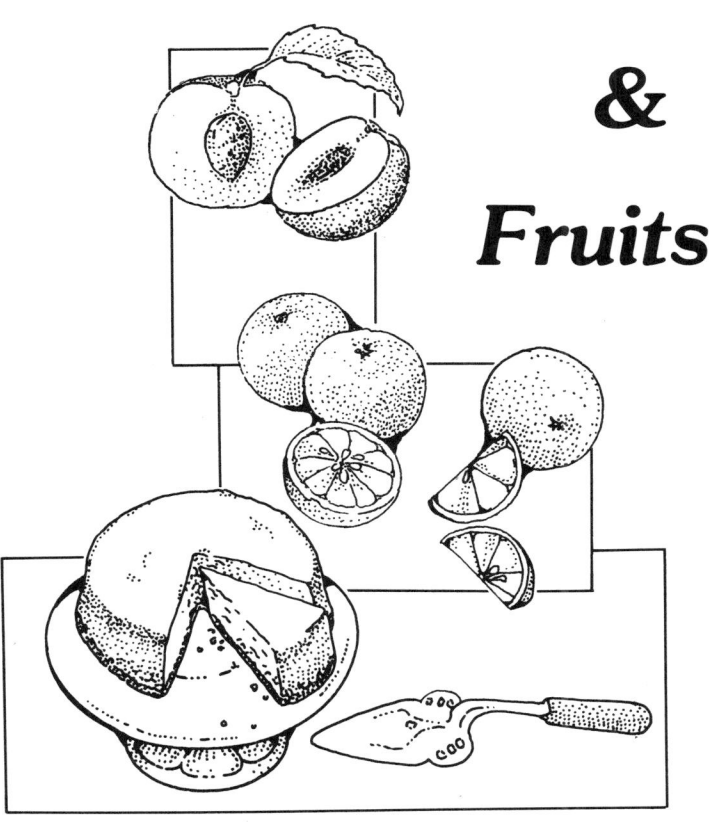

ANISE COOKIES
(Biscotti Di Anise)

½ cup margarine or oil
1 drop anise oil, OR
   1 tsp. anise extract
1 cup sugar
4 large eggs
2½ cups sifted flour
3 tsp. baking powder
1 cup chopped nuts (optional)

Mix oil and sugar; add eggs and beat until smooth. Add anise oil or extract. Sift dry ingredients together and add to egg mixture. Beat until smooth.

Grease a 10 x 15" cookie sheet. Pour mixture into cookie sheet along the LENGTHWISE edge, making two strips about 3" wide and leaving a space about 3" wide between the strips.

Bake at 350° for 15 to 18 minutes, until lightly browned. Carefully loosen each strip of the baked cookie and place on a cutting board. Cut each piece into slices about ½" wide. Scrape all the crumbs from the cookie sheet and discard. Place slices, cut side down, on the sheet. Return to the oven and bake at 375° for 7 to 10 minutes, or until lightly browned.

VARIATION: Add 1 cup raisins to the cookies.

Yields about 30 cookies.

NONNIE SAYS, "These cookies are delicious plain and are Grandpa's favorite for breakfast, dunked in coffee to start the day or in wine after dinner."

ANISE COOKIES
(Biscotti Di Anise)

½ cup margarine or oil
1 drop anise oil, OR
   1 tsp. anise extract
1 cup sugar
4 large eggs
2½ cups sifted flour
3 tsp. baking powder
1 cup chopped nuts (optional)

Mix oil and sugar; add eggs and beat until smooth. Add anise oil or extract. Sift dry ingredients together and add to egg mixture. Beat until smooth.

Grease a 10 x 15" cookie sheet. Pour mixture into cookie sheet along the LENGTHWISE edge, making two strips about 3" wide and leaving a space about 3" wide between the strips.

Bake at 350° for 15 to 18 minutes, until lightly browned. Carefully loosen each strip of the baked cookie and place on a cutting board. Cut each piece into slices about ½" wide. Scrape all the crumbs from the cookie sheet and discard. Place slices, cut side down, on the sheet. Return to the oven and bake at 375° for 7 to 10 minutes, or until lightly browned.

VARIATION: Add 1 cup raisins to the cookies.

Yields about 30 cookies.

NONNIE SAYS, "These cookies are delicious plain and are Grandpa's favorite for breakfast, dunked in coffee to start the day or in wine after dinner."

HONEY COOKIES
(Ciambelle Di Miele)

2 cups sifted flour
1½ cups honey
¼ cup oil
1½ cups chopped nuts

Place flour on a large board or table and make a well in the center. Pour honey and oil into the well and mix with a fork. Add nuts. Continue mixing and adding flour gradually until all the flour is used. Knead the dough for a few minutes until smooth.

Divide the dough into three portions and roll each portion into strips about 1" wide and 15" long. Lay the strips on a greased cookie sheet (10 x 15") and flatten strips to about 1½" wide.

Bake at 350° for 18 to 20 minutes. Remove from oven and immediately slice strips into ¼" wide cookies. Separate the cookies and let them cool on a wire rack.

VARIATION: Instead of the nuts, use 1½ tsp. (or more to taste) of black pepper. The pepper should be mixed in with the flour.

Yields about 90 cookies.

> NONNIE SAYS, "These cookies are very firm, and if the nuts and black pepper are omitted, they make a good teething cookie for babies."

JAM TART
(Crostata Di Marmellata)

1¼ cups margarine
1¼ cups sugar
4 eggs (large)
1 tsp. lemon extract
3½ cups sifted flour
1 tsp. baking powder
2 lb. jar of jam (any flavor)

In a medium bowl, cream margarine and sugar. Add lemon extract and beat until well mixed. Add the eggs, one at a time, beating well after each addition. Then add the flour and baking powder and mix until smooth.

Grease a 10 x 15" cookie sheet (the kind with sides). With hands, spread all but about 1 cup of the dough evenly in the pans, covering the bottom and about ¾" up the sides.

Spread the jam evenly on top of the dough to within ½" of the edge. Add enough flour (about 2 to 3 Tbsp.) to the reserved dough to make it firm enough to handle. Break off small pieces of the dough (about 2 Tbsp. at a time). Dust hands with flour and shape dough into strips about ¼" in diameter. Use the strips to make a lattice pattern across the top of the jam.

Bake at 350° for about 25 to 30 minutes, until dough is light golden brown. When cool, cut into 1½" squares.

Makes 70 to 80 squares.

LADY FINGERS
(Savoiardi)

4 eggs
1 cup sugar
2 cups flour
2 tsp. baking powder
¼ tsp. salt
1 tsp. vanilla

Beat eggs with sugar until creamy. Add vanilla. Sift flour, salt and baking powder together and slowly add to egg mixture. Beat until smooth.

Grease a cookie sheet and sprinkle with flour. Pour a spoonful of batter on the sheet, making an oblong shape about 1" wide and 3" long. Cookies should be about 2" apart on the cookie sheet.

Bake at 350° for about 10 minutes, or until a delicate brown.

Yields about 3 dozen cookies.

NONNIE SAYS, "These cookies keep very well and are nice for both adults and children. They may also be used for mocha cream cake."

ITALIAN CREAM
(Crema Italiana)

6 egg yolks, beaten
¼ to ½ cup sugar (to taste)
2 cups light cream
   (not half and half)
Rind of ½ lemon
1 cinnamon stick
½ tsp. vanilla (optional)

Combine all the ingredients except for vanilla in the top of a double boiler. Cook over boiling water, stirring frequently, until the mixture thickens (about 30 to 45 minutes). WATCH CAREFULLY, AS THE MIXTURE CURDLES EASILY. The cream thickens only slightly, and it is like custard sauce in consistency when cooked.

Remove from heat, add vanilla, and stir occasionally while the mixture cools. Cool thoroughly before using.

This cream can be used as a filling for cream cake or poured over fresh berries.

NOTE: Heavy or whipping cream can be used instead of the light cream for a thicker, richer cream.

Yields 2 to 2½ cups cream.

ITALIAN SPONGE CAKE
(Pane Di Spagna)

5 eggs, separated
1 cup sugar
1 Tbsp. lemon juice or vanilla
1 tsp. grated lemon rind (optional)
¼ tsp. salt
1 cup sifted flour

Beat the egg whites until they stand up in soft peaks. Beat ¼ cup of the sugar into the egg whites, a tablespoon at a time. Without washing the beater, beat the yolks with the lemon juice or vanilla until thick and lemon colored. Gradually add ¾ cup sugar and lemon rind, if desired.

Gently fold egg yolk mixture into the beaten egg whites until well blended. Sift flour and salt together and gradually fold into the egg mixture, ¼ cup at a time.

Pour into an ungreased 9" tube pan or two 9" layer pans. If using a tube pan, bake at 325° for about 1 hour; if using layer pans, bake at 350°for about ½ hour. To test, press lightly with finger. If cake is done, it will spring back.

Invert cake on a wire cake rack and let stand until cold. Loosen with a spatula and ease out of the pan.

Yields one 9" tube cake or two 9" layer cakes.

CREAM CAKE
(Zuppa Inglese)

1 sponge cake, made in two 9" layer pans
1 double recipe Italian cream
   or cream pudding
2 Tbsp. anisette
½ to ¾ cup fruit liqueur (any flavor
   or combination of flavors)
½ pint whipping cream (optional)

Using a serrated knife, cut cake layers in half horizontally to make four layers.

Place one layer on a cake plate. Mix liqueurs and sprinkle ¼ of the mixture over the cake. Spread ⅓ of the cream over the layer. Repeat the process for the remaining layers, ending with a layer of sponge cake. Sprinkle the remaining liqueur over the top of the cake.

Serve plain or dust the top layer with powdered sugar, or whip the cream and use to cover the top and sides of the cake. Decorate with candied cherries or silver dragees.

NOTE: The cake and cream should be made and assembled a day ahead of time, or early on the day it will be served, to allow the flavors to blend. After assembling, keep the cake refrigerated until eaten.

Serves 12 to 16.

CREAM PUDDING OR FILLING
(Crema)

        5 Tbsp. flour
        ¼ cup sugar
        ¼ tsp. salt
        2 cups milk, scalded
        2 eggs, beaten
        1 Tbsp. butter
        1 tsp. vanilla
        1 tsp. orange juice (optional)
        1 tsp. Amaretto liqueur (optional)

Thoroughly mix flour, sugar and salt and put in the top of a double boiler. Add scalded milk and cook until thick. Slowly add the beaten eggs and cook, stirring often, until mixture is thick and smooth. Add butter, vanilla and optional flavorings, if desired. Remove from heat and cool, stirring occasionally.

Use as a filling for cream cake, mocha cream cake, cream puffs or for any recipe calling for a cream filling.

Yields about 2 cups.

MOCHA CREAM CAKE
(Tira Mi Su)

1 lb. lady fingers
   (packaged or made from recipe in this book)
OR: two 9" sponge cakes, each split into 2 layers
1½ cups very strong coffee or espresso, cooled
1 Tbsp. Kahlua, Amaretto, or vanilla
Double recipe cream pudding or filling
3 Tbsp. cocoa
1 pint heavy cream, whipped

Place a layer of lady fingers on the bottom of a 9 x 13" glass baking pan. Be sure the entire bottom of the pan is covered with the cookies. Mix the coffee and liqueur or vanilla. Slowly pour about ⅓ of the mixture over the lady fingers, soaking them as evenly as possible. Cover with about ⅓ of the cream pudding. Sift about ⅓ of the cocoa over the pudding. Make two more layers with the remaining lady fingers, coffee mixture, cream and cocoa.

Cover and refrigerate 3 or 4 hours, until mixture is set. Just before serving, cover with the whipping cream.

Serves 12.

POUND CAKE
(Ciambellone)

1¼ cup sugar
½ cup shortening
3 eggs
3 cups flour
3 tsp. baking powder
dash of salt
1 cup milk
1 lemon rind, grated
3 tsp. lemon juice
1 Tbsp. anise seeds (optional)

   Cream sugar and shortening, add eggs and beat well. Sift dry ingredients together. Add dry ingredients to egg mixture, alternating with milk. Add flavorings and mix well. Pour into a greased 9 or 10" tube pan. Bake at 350° for 50 to 55 minutes.

Yields one 9 or 10" cake.

CANNOLI

1 cup flour
¼ tsp. salt
1 Tbsp. sugar
1 Tbsp. oil
¼ cup white wine
2 cups oil (or more) for deep frying

Place flour in a mound on pastry board or in a large bowl. Make a well in the center and add salt, sugar, oil and wine. Stir with a fork until mixture is well blended. Gradually stir in flour until a stiff dough is formed. Knead until smooth. Roll out on a floured board until about 1/8" thick. Cut dough into 4" squares.

Wrap squares around cannoli tubes and press edges together (moisten edges of dough with a little water to make them stick together).

Heat oil in a deep pan. Gently lower cannoli shells (tube and all) into oil and brown evenly. Using tongs, **VERY CAREFULLY** remove the metal tube before the shells are completely browned so that the insides of the shells can brown also. Drain on paper towels and cool completely before filling. Cannoli shells (without filling) can be kept in a covered container for several days.

Yields 12 shells.

FILLING:

2 cups ricotta
¼ cup sugar
2 Tbsp. candied fruit, finely chopped (optional)
2 Tbsp. chocolate, chopped
1 to 2 tsp. anisette
powdered sugar (optional)

Mix all the ingredients (except powdered sugar) well. Just before serving, use a pastry tube or teaspoon to put filling into shells. Sprinkle with powdered sugar, if desired.

Serves 12.

RICOTTA PIE CRUST
(La Crosta Per Casatella)

1 cup flour
6 Tbsp. shortening
1 large egg, separated
¼ tsp. salt
2 Tbsp. sugar
1 to 2 Tbsp. cold water

Cut shortening into the flour to make pieces the size of small peas. Add the egg yolk, salt, sugar and just enough water to hold the dough together.

Press the dough evenly into a 9" pie pan, OR: roll the dough out between sheets of lightly floured waxed paper.

Beat the egg white lightly. Cover surface of dough with the egg white and then add ricotta filling.

Bake according to directions included with the ricotta pie recipe.

Yields one 9" pie crust.

EASTER BREAD
(Pane Di Pasqua)

1 envelope dry yeast
½ tsp. sugar
½ cup lukewarm water
¾ cup sugar
1 tsp. salt
½ cup margarine, softened
3 eggs (at room temperature), beaten
5½ to 6 cups sifted flour
1 tsp. anise extract
1 tsp. vanilla
1½ tsp. anise seeds (optional)
½ tsp. cinnamon
2 whole eggs, with shells, for decoration

In a small bowl, dissolve yeast and ½ tsp. sugar in water. In a large bowl, combine sugar, salt, beaten eggs, margarine and flavorings. When yeast mixture bubbles, add to the sugar and egg mixture. Mix well. Beat in about 2½ cups of the flour. Stir until well blended.

Gradually add the remaining flour, mixing until the dough becomes too stiff to stir with a spoon. Turn the dough out on a floured board and knead for about 10 minutes, until smooth and elastic, adding a little more flour if necessary. Put the dough in a bowl greased with oil, turn the dough to grease it on all sides, and cover with a towel.

Let the dough rise in a warm place for 2½ to 3 hours or until double in bulk. Grease two 9" round baking pans. Punch the dough down and shape into 2 round loaves. Put an uncooked egg (with shell) in the center of each loaf and push into loaf enough for the egg to stay in place. (The egg will be hard cooked and good to eat after baking.)

Let the loaves rise in a warm place until double in bulk (the dough rises slowly). Bake at 350° for 25 to 30 minutes. Rub the top of the loaves with butter as soon as they are removed from the oven.

Yields 2 loaves.

FRESH PEACHES IN WINE
(Pesche Fresche Al Vino)

4 large ripe peaches
2 cups wine, rosé or red

Peel peaches and cut into bite-sized sections. Put in bowl and add wine. Allow flavors to blend for about one hour before serving. Can be chilled or served at room temperature.

Peaches and wine can be kept for a day or two in the refrigerator. Peaches will discolor slightly and take on the color of the wine, but this does not affect the quality of the peaches—and it gives them a very nice flavor.

NOTE: Canned peaches may be used in place of fresh peaches. Use with or without the syrup.

Serves 4.

FRIED APPLES
(Mele Fritte)

3 large, firm apples, peeled, cored,
 and cut into slices ¼" thick

1 pkg. dry yeast
1¼ cups water
1½ cups flour
1 Tbsp. oil
oil for frying

Dissolve yeast in warm water. Add flour and oil and mix with a spoon or beater (dough will be loose, similar to a pancake batter). Let the dough rise in warm place for about 20 minutes. When dough has doubled in size, stir it down and let rest a few minutes.

Dip apple slices in dough and fry in hot oil.

ALTERNATE DOUGH:

1½ cups flour
1 cup milk
1 egg
1 tsp. baking powder
oil for frying

Mix flour, milk, egg, and baking powder together. The mixture should be about the consistency of pancake batter.

Cover the bottom of a deep pan with about 1" of oil and heat until hot enough for frying. Dip apple slices in the batter to cover completely and fry until golden on both sides.

Serves 4.

BOW TIES OR HONEY BALL CLUSTERS
(Frappe Or Struffoli)

2 cups flour
pinch of salt
1 Tbsp. sugar
3 large eggs
¼ lb. margarine, softened
1 cup (or more) oil for frying

Sift flour into a large mixing bowl or on a board. Make a well in the center and add salt, sugar, eggs and margarine. Beat with a fork or your fingertips. Gradually beat in all the flour to make a stiff dough. Knead dough until smooth. Cover dough with a bowl or clean cloth and let rest for about 10 minutes.

TO MAKE BOW TIES:

Cut off about a 1-cup size piece of dough. Place dough on a floured board and roll into a circle about ⅛" thick. With a cutting wheel or knife, cut into strips about 1" wide. Shape into bow ties or knots. To make bow ties, cut strip about 4" long and pinch together in the middle to form bow ties. To make knots, cut strip about 6" long and tie into loose knots. Fry in hot oil, as described below.

TO MAKE HONEY BALLS:

Divide dough in half. Place the dough on a lightly floured board and roll into a rectangle ¼ to ½" thick. Cut rolled dough into strips ½" wide. Roll each portion between the palms of your hands or on a lightly floured board to form a "rope" about ¼ to ½" thick. Cut the "ropes" into pieces about ½" long. Spread apart to keep from sticking. Fry in hot oil as described below.

FRYING DIRECTIONS: Heat 2 inches of oil or shortening in a deep kettle or fryer. Test by dropping a small strip of dough (about 1" long) into the hot fat. If it rises quickly to the top and browns lightly without scorching, the fat is ready.

Use a slotted spoon to gently lower shaped dough into hot fat, being careful not to add too many at one time. Stir gently with the slotted spoon to brown evenly on all sides. When a light golden brown, remove with a slotted spoon and drain on paper towels.

TO SERVE: The bow ties can be sprinkled with sifted powdered sugar, or with honey-lemon syrup, lemon syrup or with honey syrup (recipes follow).

The balls can be added to honey lemon syrup or honey syrup, stirring until all are coated with syrup. After the balls are coated with syrup, wet hands and shape balls into a ring on a serving plate. Sprinkle with colored sugar candies or slivered toasted almonds (almonds can also be added to syrup with the balls).

Serves 8 to 10.

HONEY SAUCE

1 cup honey
3 Tbsp. sugar

Put honey in a small saucepan and sprinkle sugar over it until sugar is absorbed.

Bring mixture to a boil and boil gently for about 5 minutes. While the mixture is warm, pour over the fried dough shapes (the mixture becomes too thick to pour if allowed to cool).

Yields about 1 cup.

HONEY LEMON SAUCE

½ cup honey
½ cup sugar
1 to 2 lemons
grated lemon rind (optional)

Squeeze lemons. Combine all ingredients in a saucepan. Heat slowly until the mixture boils and let boil for about 1 minute, stirring constantly. While the mixture is warm, pour over fried dough shapes (the mixture becomes too thick to pour when allowed to cool).

Yields about ½ cup.

LEMON SAUCE

½ cup lemon juice
¼ cup sugar

Combine ingredients in a pan and bring to a boil. Boil for 10 to 15 minutes, stirring frequently. When mixture begins to turn golden in color, remove from heat, even if it seems too runny. Cool slightly and pour over fried dough shapes.

Yields ½ cup.

MIXED FRUIT WITH GRAND MARNIER
(Frutta Con Grand Marnier)

4 cups mixed fruit
 (strawberries, peaches, bananas,
 pears, melons)
¼ cup sugar
¼ cup Grand Marnier

Cut the fruit into bite-sized pieces. Mix in sugar and then add Grand Marnier. Let stand for at least ½ hour before serving to blend flavors.

Serves 4 to 6.

ROAST CHESTNUTS
(Castagne Arrostite)

1 lb. chestnuts
 (bought at a food store,
  NOT chestnuts from local trees)

Using a sharp paring knife, make a gash through the skin of each chestnut (the gash is important, since the chestnuts will "explode" when heated if this is not done).

Place the chestnuts in a single layer on a cookie sheet. Bake at 325° for about 45 to 50 minutes, or until the inside of the chestnut is cooked to taste.

TO SERVE: Let each person peel the tough outer skin and eat the tasty inside of the chestnut. They need no seasoning or flavoring. Roast chestnuts are delicious hot, warm or cold.

Serves 6.

STEWED CHESTNUTS
(Castagne Stufate)

1 lb. chestnuts
1 bay leaf

Make a gash in each chestnut. Place chestnuts in a pan and cover with water. Add bay leaf.

Cook, covered, over low heat for about 45 minutes, or until the chestnuts are cooked to taste. Drain, remove skins and serve warm or at room temperature.

Serves 6.

NONNIE SAYS, "Chestnuts are traditionally served after a meal, with wine. They can also be served as a snack or used for stuffing, for fruit salad or fruit cocktail, or for baking. Chestnuts are not only tasty, but they are easy to digest."

Leonardi's
INTERNATIONAL RESTAURANT

2861 East Commercial Boulevard
Ft. Lauderdale, Florida 33308
(305) 772-3710

The influence of his mother's cooking helped Robert Leonardi develop a love of fine food and wine and also led him to the restaurant business. He opened Leonardi's International as a wine and cheese store in 1976, but soon expanded to include gourmet foods and catering for small parties. The freshly prepared specialties became so popular that Leonardi's began to serve lunches and dinners, and the catering business flourished at the same time.

In 1987 Leonardi's was completely renovated and expanded. The new restaurant features a wine bar, a large main dining room and four smaller rooms suitable for private parties. The restaurant continues to offer fine foods, freshly prepared daily on the premises. Gourmet foods, homemade favorites and fine wines are still offered in the retail store.

The catering operation now provides a wide variety of services, from casual gatherings to formal events, corporate entertaining, yacht parties, wedding receptions and many other events serving up to several thousand people. Robert Leonardi continues to personally supervise both the catering and restaurant operations.

A few of the many dishes featured on the menu at Leonardi's International are included on the following pages. In addition to the foods included here, a Leonardi chef will also prepare any of the recipes in this cookbook, provided the restaurant is notified at least 24 hours in advance.

PESTO SAUCE

3 to 4 cloves garlic
3 cups fresh basil leaves
½ cup pine nuts
½ cup grated Romano cheese
½ cup olive oil
½ lb. pasta

Mince the basil, garlic and pine nuts. Slowly add the oil until the mixture is smooth. Add grated cheese and blend well. Heat until mixture is just warm.

Pour over cooked spaghetti or angel hair pasta (angel hair requires more sauce). Serve immediately.

Serves 2.

VEAL POMODORO

1 lb. veal scallopine, or very thinly sliced veal
½ cup flour (for coating)
½ cup olive oil
1 tsp. minced garlic
1 tsp. red pepper flakes
   (or less, according to taste)
½ dozen vine ripe tomatoes,
   peeled and quartered
½ cup chopped fresh basil
½ cup dry white wine
½ cup veal stock or beef bouillon

Cut veal into serving pieces. Dip in flour and then saute in olive oil until cooked. Set aside.

Saute garlic and red pepper in oil remaining in pan for about 10 to 20 seconds. Add tomatoes, white wine, basil and veal stock. Add salt and pepper to taste. Add veal to sauce and saute for about two minutes. Serve with fresh pasta.

Serves 4.

FETTUCINI LEONARDI'S

2 cups heavy cream
4 Tbsp. sweet butter
3 tsp. salt
pinch freshly grated nutmeg
1 Tbsp. grated imported Parmesan cheese
1½ to 2 cups glazed poached salmon
   (skin and bones removed)
5 Tbsp. chopped fresh dill
1 lb. fresh fettucini
dill sprigs for garnish

Bring the cream and half the butter to a simmer in a small saucepan. Add 1 tsp. of the salt and the nutmeg and continue to simmer until the cream is reduced by about one third.

Bring 4 quarts water to a boil in a large pot. Add remaining 2 tsp. salt, and then the fettucini.

Meanwhile, stir grated Parmesan cheese, then the flaked salmon and the dill into the cream and remove from heat.

Drain fettucini, return it to the hot pan and toss with remaining butter until butter is melted. Place the pasta on a serving patter, cover with the cream mixture and toss lightly. Garnish with sprigs of dill. Serve immediately.

Serves 4.

PASTA PRIMAVERA

7 Tbsp. unsalted butter
4 shallots, minced
2 carrots, peeled and diced
½ cup champagne or dry white wine
1½ cups heavy cream
3 Tbsp. chopped fresh basil
1 Tbsp. chopped fresh tarragon
2 cups diagonally cut 1" pieces
 fresh asparagus
2 leeks, well rinsed, dried, and cut into
 fine julienne strips
8 ounces fresh shiitake mushrooms,
 rinsed, dried and sliced
1½ cups fresh shelled peas
¾ cups crumbled Parmesan cheese
1 lb. hot cooked pasta

Melt 5 Tbsp. of the butter in a large pan over medium heat. Add the shallots and saute for 5 minutes. Stir in the carrots and cook for 3 minutes. Add the champagne, heavy cream, basil and tarragon. Cook until thickened to a good coating consistency, about 15 minutes.

Meanwhile, cook the asparagus in boiling, salted water until tender but firm. Blanch the leeks in boiling water for 1 minute. Saute the mushrooms in the remaining 2 Tbsp. butter.

When the sauce is thickened, stir in asparagus, half the leeks, the mushrooms and peas. Simmer over low heat for a few minutes. Season to taste with salt and pepper and stir in cheese. Spoon over pasta. Garnish with remaining leeks. Serve immediately.

Serves 4.

BOLOGNESE SAUCE

2 pounds ground beef
½ cup unsalted butter
1 large yellow onion, diced into ½" pieces
1 medium green pepper, seeded, cored and diced
2 ribs celery, diced into ¼" pieces
2 cans (28 oz.) Italian plum tomatoes
1 bay leaf
3 Tbsp. dried oregano
2 Tbsp. dried basil
2 tsp. salt
1 tsp. freshly ground black pepper
1 cup dry red wine
2 cans (6 oz.) tomato paste
⅛ tsp. fennel seed

Brown ground beef in a skillet over medium heat. Drain, set aside.

Melt butter in a large saucepan over medium heat. Add the onion, green pepper and celery and saute until limp, about 5 minutes. Stir in beef, tomatoes (with liquid), bay leaf, oregano, basil, salt and pepper. Simmer, covered, for 30 to 40 minutes. Stir in the wine, tomato paste and fennel seed and simmer, covered, for 15 minutes.

Let stand at least 30 minutes before serving, but preferably overnight. Reheat before serving. Yields enough for about 2 lbs. of pasta.

Serves 8.

TRADITIONAL HOLIDAY DINNER MENUS

CHRISTMAS EVE
(Vigilia di Natale)

Antipasto

Spaghetti with Clam Sauce

Italian Wine

Fried Smelts Squid Baked Fish

Fried Apples Fried Mixed Vegetables

Lettuce Salad

Assorted Italian Cookies Nuts and Fruit

Espresso Liqueurs

CHRISTMAS DAY
(Natale)

Antipasto

Chicken Soup with Beaten Eggs

Baked Pasta

Italian Wine

Fried Veal Cutlet Fried Mushrooms Rice Balls

Roast Chicken Roast Peppers

Lettuce Salad

Cream Cake Assorted Nuts and Fruit

Espresso Liqueurs

NEW YEAR'S EVE

(Vigilia di C'apo D'Anno)

Antipasto

Lentil Soup

Sausage and Peppers   Potato Salad, Italian Style

Italian Wine

Lettuce Salad

Bow Ties and Honey Balls   Roast Chestnuts and Fruit

Espresso   Liqueurs

NEW YEAR'S DAY

(C'apo D'Anno)

Antipasto

Chicken Soup with Pastina

Roast Chicken and Potatoes

Italian Wine

String Beans with Oil and Garlic

Lettuce Salad

Bow Ties and Honey Balls   Assorted Italian Cookies

Roast Chestnuts and Fruit

Espresso   Liqueurs

MARDI GRAS
(Carnevale)

Sausage   Roast Chicken and Potatoes   Fried Peppers

Italian Wine

Lettuce Salad

Assorted Italian Cookies   Roast Chestnuts

Espresso   Liqueurs

EASTER SUNDAY
(Pasqua)

Antipasto

Chicken Soup with Beaten Eggs

Homemade Macaroni with Tomato Meat Sauce

Roast Beef

Italian Wine

Mixed Fried Vegetables

Lettuce Salad

Ricotta Pie   Fruit

Espresso   Liqueurs

Index

ANCHOVY SALAD	92
ANISE COOKIES	101
APPETIZER SALAD	91
APPLES, FRIED	117
ARTICHOKES WITH OIL AND OREGANO	61
ASPARAGUS WITH OIL AND GARLIC	62
BAKED EGG NOODLES	17
BAKED FISH	54
BAKED PASTA	18
BAKED STUFFED MUSHROOMS	64
BAKED ZUCCHINI	63
BEAN SOUP WITH PASTA	5
BEEF, ROAST	43
BEEF, STUFFED	44
BEETS WITH FRESH HERBS	65
BOLOGNESE SAUCE	133
BOW TIES OR HONEY BALL CLUSTERS	118
BREAD, EASTER	115
BREADED CHICKEN BREASTS	37
BROCCOLI, WITH PASTA	20
CABBAGE WITH TOMATOES	66
CAKE, CREAM	108
CAKE, MOCHA CREAM	110
CAKE, POUND	111
CAKE, SPONGE	107
CANNOLI	112
CAULIFLOWER WITH PARSLEY	67
CHEESE PIZZA	11
CHESTNUTS, ROAST	122
CHESTNUTS, STEWED	123
CHICKEN BREASTS, BREADED	37
CHICKEN BREASTS, SAUTEED WITH WINE	41
CHICKEN SOUP	3
CHICKEN SOUP WITH BEATEN EGGS	4
CHICKEN WITH PEPPERS	38

CHICKEN WITH PEPPERS AND TOMATOES	39
CHICKEN, ROAST	40
CLAM SAUCE AND SPAGHETTI	28
COOKIES, ANISE	101
COOKIES, HONEY	102
COOKIES, WINE	105
CORN MEAL	22
CREAM CAKE	108
CREAM PUDDING OR FILLING	109
CREAM, ITALIAN	106
DANDELION SALAD	93
EASTER BREAD	115
EGG NOODLES, BAKED	17
EGGPLANT PARMIGIANA	69
EGGPLANT, FRIED	68
EGGPLANT, MARINATED	73
EGGPLANT, STUFFED.	84
EGGS WITH TOMATOES	70
ESCAROLE, SAUTEED	80
FETTUCINI LEONARDI'S	131
FISH, BAKED	54
FRESH PEACHES IN WINE	116
FRESH TOMATO SALAD	94
FRIED APPLES	117
FRIED EGGPLANT	68
FRIED PEPPERS	71
FRIED PIZZA DOUGH	12
FRIED SMELTS	55
FRIED ZUCCHINI BLOSSOMS	72
FRUIT, WITH GRAND MARNIER	121
HOMEMADE PASTA	23
HOMEMADE SAUSAGE	48
HONEY AND LEMON SAUCES	120
HONEY COOKIES	102
ITALIAN CREAM	106
ITALIAN SPONGE CAKE	107
JAM TART	103
LADY FINGERS	104
LENTIL SOUP	6

LETTUCE SALAD	95
LIVER AND ONIONS	53
MACARONI AND CHEESE	19
MANICOTTI	24
MARINATED EGGPLANT	73
MARINATED STEAK	42
MEATBALLS	46
MIXED DEEP FRIED VEGETABLES	74
MIXED FRUIT WITH GRAND MARNIER	121
MOCHA CREAM CAKE	110
MOZZARELLA SANDWICH	8
MUSHROOM MARINARA SAUCE	29
MUSHROOMS WITH GARLIC AND PARSLEY	75
MUSHROOMS, STUFFED	64
ONIONS, SAUTEED	81
OPEN FACED CHEESE SANDWICH	9
ORANGE SALAD	96
OVEN FRIED POTATOES	76
PASTA PRIMAVERA	132
PASTA WITH BROCCOLI	20
PASTA, BAKED	18
PASTA, HOMEMADE	23
PEA SOUP	7
PEACHES, IN WINE	116
PEPPERS, AND SAUSAGE	49
PEPPERS, AND VEAL	51
PEPPERS, FRIED	71
PEPPERS, ROAST	79
PEPPERS, STUFFED	47
PESTO SAUCE	129
PIE, RICOTTA	113
PIZZA DOUGH	10
PIZZA DOUGH, FRIED	12
PIZZA, CHEESE	11
PIZZA, WHITE	13
POTATO DUMPLINGS	21
POTATO SALAD WITH STRING BEANS AND TOMATOES	97
POTATO SALAD, ITALIAN STYLE	98

POTATOES, OVEN FRIED	76
POUND CAKE	111
PUDDING, CREAM	109
RADISHES AND OIL	77
RAPI	78
RICE BALLS	25
RICE SALAD	26
RICOTTA PIE	113
RICOTTA PIE CRUST	114
ROAST BEEF	43
ROAST CHESTNUTS	122
ROAST CHICKEN AND POTATOES	40
ROAST PEPPERS	79
SALAD, ANCHOVY	92
SALAD, FRESH TOMATO	94
SALAD, LETTUCE	95
SALAD, ORANGE	96
SALAD, POTATO WITH STRING BEANS	97
SALAD, POTATO, ITALIAN STYLE	98
SALAD, RICE	26
SALAD, STRING BEAN	83
SALAD, DANDELION	93
SALMON CROQUETTES	56
SANDWICH, CHEESE AND TOMATO	9
SANDWICH, MOZZARELLA	8
SAUCE, BOLOGNESE	133
SAUCE, CLAM	28
SAUCE, MUSHROOM	29
SAUCE, PESTO	129
SAUCE, TOMATO	30
SAUCE, TOMATO MEAT	33
SAUCE, TUNA FISH	32
SAUSAGE AND PEPPERS	49
SAUSAGE, HOMEMADE	48
SAUTEED CHICKEN BREASTS WITH WINE	41
SAUTEED ESCAROLE OR ENDIVE	80
SAUTEED ONIONS	81
SAUTEED ZUCCHINI	86
SCALLOPS	57

SMELTS, FRIED	55
SOUP, BEAN	5
SOUP, CHICKEN	3
SOUP, CHICKEN WITH BEATEN EGGS	4
SOUP, LENTIL	6
SOUP, PEA	7
SPAGHETTI WITH GARLIC AND OIL	31
SPAGHETTI, AND CLAM SAUCE	28
SPAGHETTI, AND TUNA FISH SAUCE	32
SQUID	58
STEAK, MARINATED	42
STEAK, THIN	45
STEW, VEAL	52
STEWED CHESTNUTS	123
STRING BEAN SALAD	83
STRING BEANS WITH OIL AND GARLIC	82
STUFFED EGGPLANT	84
STUFFED PEPPERS	47
STUFFED ROLLED BEEF	44
STUFFED TOMATOES	27
SWISS CHARD WITH TOMATO SAUCE	85
THIN STEAK	45
TOMATO MEAT SAUCE	33
TOMATO SAUCE	30
TOMATOES, STUFFED	27
TUNA FISH SAUCE AND SPAGHETTI	32
VEAL AND PEPPERS	51
VEAL PARMESAN	50
VEAL POMODORO	130
VEAL STEW	52
VEGETABLES, FRIED	74
WHITE PIZZA	13
WINE COOKIES	105
ZUCCHINI BLOSSOMS, FRIED	72
ZUCCHINI, BAKED	63
ZUCCHINI, PEPPERS, ONIONS AND TOMATOES	87
ZUCCHINI, SAUTEED	86

From Nonnie's Italian Kitchen

Compiled and edited by
Elmerina Leonardi Parkman
and Norma Leonardi Leone

Additional copies of this book may be
ordered directly from the publisher.

To order, fill out the form below and send to:

Lion Press
P. O. Box 92541
Rochester, NY 14692

Other Books Available From Lion Press:

YOUR CHILD AND X-RAYS $8.95
A Parent's Guide to Radiation, X-rays and Other Imaging Procedures

A MOTHER'S GUIDE TO COMPUTERS $ 5.95

Please send _____ copies of YOUR CHILD AND X-RAYS $8.95

_____ copies of A MOTHER'S GUIDE TO COMPUTERS $5.95

_____ copies of From NONNIE'S ITALIAN KITCHEN $8.95

Enclosed _____ for books, plus $ 1.50 for shipping for the first book and 50 cents for each additional book (New York State residents add 7% tax).

Please type or print clearly:

NAME: _____

ADDRESS: _____

CITY: _____

STATE: _____ ZIP: _____

Notes

Notes